June 2013

# INSURANCE MARKETS

# Impacts of and Regulatory Response to the 2007-2009 Financial Crisis

GAO-13-583

# INSURANCE MARKETS

## Impacts of and Regulatory Response to the 2007-2009 Financial Crisis

Highlights of GAO-13-583, a report to congressional requesters

## Why GAO Did This Study

Insurance plays an important role in ensuring the smooth functioning of the economy. Concerns about the oversight of the $1 trillion life and property/casualty insurance industry arose during the 2007-2009 financial crisis, when one of the largest holding companies, AIG, suffered severe losses that threatened to affect its insurance subsidiaries. GAO was asked to examine any effects of the financial crisis on the insurance industry.

This report addresses (1) what is known about how the financial crisis of 2007-2009 affected the insurance industry and policyholders, (2) the factors that affected the impact of the crisis on insurers and policyholders, and (3) the types of actions that have been taken since the crisis to help prevent or mitigate potential negative effects of future economic downturns on insurance companies and their policyholders.

To do this work, GAO analyzed insurance industry financial data from 2002 through 2011 and interviewed a range of industry observers, participants, and regulators.

View GAO-13-583. For more information, contact Alicia Puente Cackley (202) 512-8678 or cackleya@gao.gov.

## What GAO Found

The effects of the financial crisis on insurers and policyholders were generally limited, with a few exceptions. While some insurers experienced capital and liquidity pressures in 2008, their capital levels had recovered by the end of 2009 (see figure). Net income also dropped but recovered somewhat in 2009. Effects on insurers' investments, underwriting performance, and premium revenues were also limited. However, some life insurers that offered variable annuities with guaranteed living benefits, as well as financial and mortgage guaranty insurers, were more affected by their exposures to the distressed equity and mortgage markets. The crisis had a generally minor effect on policyholders, but some mortgage and financial guaranty policyholders—banks and other commercial entities—received partial claims or faced decreased availability of coverage.

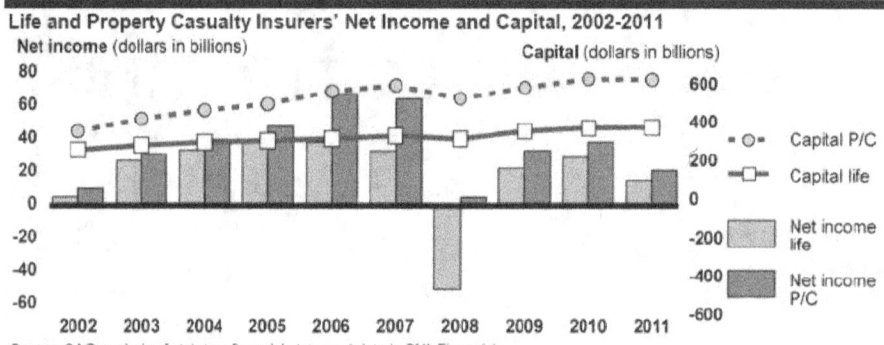

**Life and Property Casualty Insurers' Net Income and Capital, 2002-2011**

Source: GAO analysis of statutory financial statement data in SNL Financial.

Note: Data are shown in nominal dollars (i.e., unadjusted for inflation).

Actions by state and federal regulators and the National Association of Insurance Commissioners (NAIC), among other factors, helped limit the effects of the crisis. First, state insurance regulators shared more information with each other to focus their oversight activities. In response to transparency issues highlighted by American International Group, Inc.'s securities lending program, NAIC required more detailed reports from insurers. Also, a change in methodology by NAIC to help better reflect the value of certain securities also reduced the risk-based capital some insurers had to hold. To further support insurers' capital levels, some states and NAIC also changed reporting requirements for certain assets. These changes affected insurers' capital levels for regulatory purposes, but rating agency officials said they did not have a significant effect on insurers' financial condition. Several federal programs also provided support to qualified insurers. Finally, insurance business practices, regulatory restrictions, and a low interest rate environment helped reduce the effects of the crisis.

NAIC and state regulators' efforts since the crisis have included an increased focus on insurers' risks and capital adequacy, and oversight of noninsurance entities in group holding company structures. The Own Risk and Solvency Assessment, an internal assessment of insurers' business plan risks, will apply to most insurers and is expected to take effect in 2015. NAIC also amended its Insurance Holding Company System Regulatory Act to address the issues of transparency and oversight of holding company entities. However, most states have yet to adopt the revisions, and implementation could take several years.

_____ **United States Government Accountability Office**

# Contents

## Figures

## Abbreviations

| | |
|---|---|
| ABS | asset-backed securities |
| ACL | authorized control level |
| AIG | American International Group, Inc. |
| AMBUL | A.M. Best's U.S. Life Insurance Index |
| AMBUPC | A.M. Best's U.S. Property Casualty Insurance Index |
| CDO | collateralized debt obligations |
| CFPB | Bureau of Consumer Financial Protection |
| CMBS | commercial mortgage-backed security |
| DTA | deferred tax asset |
| EESA | Emergency Economic Stabilization Act of 2008 |
| FAWG | Financial Analysis Working Group |
| FIO | Federal Insurance Office |
| FHFA | Federal Housing Finance Agency |
| GLB | guaranteed living benefits |
| IAIS | International Association of Insurance Supervisors |
| MBS | mortgage-backed securities |
| NAIC | National Association of Insurance Commissioners |
| NYA | NYSE Composite Index |
| NYSE | New York Stock Exchange |
| ORSA | Own Risk and Solvency Assessment |
| P/C | property and casualty |
| RBC | risk-based capital |
| RMBS | residential mortgage-backed security |
| SIFI | systemically important financial institution |
| SMI | Solvency Modernization Initiative |
| SPV | special purpose vehicle |
| SSAP | Statement of Statutory Accounting Principles |
| TARP | Troubled Asset Relief Program |

# GAO

U.S. GOVERNMENT ACCOUNTABILITY OFFICE

441 G St. N.W.
Washington, DC 20548

June 27, 2013

The Honorable Randy Neugebauer
Chairman
Subcommittee on Housing and Insurance
Committee on Financial Services
House of Representatives

The Honorable Steve Stivers
House of Representatives

The U.S. life and property/casualty (P/C) insurance industries wrote over $1 trillion in total premiums in 2011 and play an important role in ensuring the smooth functioning of the economy. Concerns about the oversight of the insurance industry arose during the 2007-2009 financial crisis, when one of the largest U.S. holding companies that had substantial insurance operations, American International Group, Inc. (AIG), suffered large losses. These losses were driven in large part by activities conducted by a non-insurance affiliate, AIG Financial Products, but also included securities lending activity undertaken by some of its life insurance companies which created liquidity issues for some insurers. The losses threatened to bankrupt the company, and AIG was one of the largest recipients of assistance by the Federal Reserve Bank of New York and the federal government under the Troubled Asset Relief Program (TARP) set up during the crisis.[1] Some other insurance companies also took advantage of federal assistance, raising concerns about their financial

---

[1]The Federal Reserve, through its emergency powers under section 13(3) of the Federal Reserve Act, and Treasury, through the Emergency Economic Stabilization Act of 2008 (EESA), which authorized the Troubled Asset Relief Program (TARP), collaborated to make available more than $180 billion for the benefit of AIG. EESA, Pub. L. No. 110-343, Div. A,122 Stat. 3765 (2008), *codified, as amended*, at 12 U.S.C. §§ 5201 et seq. EESA was enacted on October 3, 2008. EESA originally authorized Treasury to purchase or guarantee up to $700 billion in troubled assets. The Helping Families Save Their Homes Act of 2009, Pub. L. No. 111-22, Div. A, 123 Stat. 1632 (2009), amended EESA to reduce the maximum allowable amount of outstanding troubled assets under EESA by almost $1.3 billion, from $700 billion to $698.741 billion. The Dodd-Frank Wall Street Reform and Consumer Protection Act, Pub. L. No. 111-203, 124 Stat. 1376 (2010), (1) further reduced Treasury's authority to purchase or insure troubled assets to a maximum of $475 billion and (2) proh bited Treasury, under EESA, from incurring any additional obligations for a program or initiative unless the program or initiative had already been initiated prior to June 25, 2010.

position and regulators' response to and preparation for future financial crises that might affect insurers and their policyholders.

The report responds to your request to examine any effects of the financial crisis on the insurance industry and policyholders. The report addresses (1) what is known about how the financial crisis affected insurance industry and policyholders, (2) the factors that affected the impact of the crisis on insurers and policyholders, and (3) the types of actions that have been taken since the crisis to help prevent or mitigate potential negative effects of future economic downturns on insurance companies and their policyholders.[2]

For all objectives, we reviewed relevant laws and regulations, conducted a literature search and reviewed literature and past GAO reports on the financial crisis. To address how the financial crisis affected the insurance industry and policyholders, we consulted academic papers, government reports, industry representatives, and regulatory officials to identify the key characteristics associated with the financial crisis. We obtained and analyzed financial data from a variety of data sources including SNL Financial, a private financial database that contains publicly filed regulatory and financial reports, the Global Receivership Information Database from the National Association of Insurance Commissioners (NAIC), and A.M. Best's U.S. Life Insurance Index (AMBUL) and U.S. Property Casualty Insurance Index (AMBUPC). We determined that the data reviewed were sufficiently reliable for our purposes. To assess reliability, we compared select data reported in individual companies' annual financial statements to that reported in SNL Financial. We also obtained information from A.M. Best and NAIC staff about their internal controls and procedures for data collection.

To address the factors that affected the impact of the crisis on insurers and policyholders and insurance regulatory actions taken during and since the crisis, we reviewed and analyzed relevant state guidance, NAIC's model investment act, reports and documents such as the Statements of Statutory Accounting Principles, information on securities lending and permitted practices and the Solvency Modernization Initiative including associated guidance manuals and model laws such as the

---

[2]This report focuses on the life and property/casualty (P/C) insurance sectors and does not review activities within the health insurance industry.

Insurance Holding Company System Regulatory Act. We reviewed our prior work and other sources to identify federal programs that were available to insurance companies to increase access to capital. Appendix I contains additional information on our scope and methodology.

We conducted this performance audit from June 2012 to June 2013 in accordance with generally accepted government auditing standards. Those standards require that we plan and perform the audit to obtain sufficient, appropriate evidence to provide a reasonable basis for our findings and conclusions based on our audit objectives. We believe that the evidence obtained provides a reasonable basis for our findings and conclusions based on our audit objectives.

# Background

## Insurance Industry Overview

Generally, insurers offer several lines, or types, of insurance to consumers and others. Some types of insurance include life and annuity products and P/C.[3] An insurance policy can include coverage for individuals or families, ("personal lines,") and coverage for businesses, ("commercial lines"). Personal lines include home owners, renters, and automobile coverage. Commercial lines may include general liability, commercial property, and product liability insurance. The U.S. life and P/C industries wrote, or sold, an annual average of $601 billion and $472 billion, respectively, in premiums from 2002 through 2011. Figures 1 and 2 illustrate the percentage of premiums written for selected lines of insurance, compared to total premiums written in the life and P/C industries, for that time period.[4] Overall, individual annuities made up the largest portion of business (32 percent) in the life industry, while private passenger auto liability insurance was the largest portion of business (20

---

[3]P/C insurance provides protections from risk in two basic areas: protection for physical items such as houses, cars, commercial buildings and inventory (property), and protection against legal liability (casualty). Property insurance is coverage for losses related to a policyholder's own person/property. Casualty (or liability) insurance is coverage for a policyholder's legal obligations against losses the policyholder may cause to others.

[4]Premiums refer to direct (gross) written premiums registered on the books of an insurer or a reinsurer at the time a policy is issued and paid for. For life insurers, premiums also include annuity considerations, which are single or periodic payments made to purchase an annuity.

percent) in the P/C industry.[5] In the P/C industry, financial and mortgage guaranty insurance represented less than 2 percent of premiums written on average during the period.[6] These lines differ from the other P/C lines we reviewed because they facilitate liquidity in the capital markets. By protecting investors against defaults in the underlying securities, financial and mortgage guaranty insurance can support better market access and greater ease of transaction execution.

---

[5]An annuity is a contract sold by insurance companies that pays a regular income benefit for the life of one or more persons, or for a specified period of time. Types of annuities include fixed annuities, which have rates that can change periodically but will never be below a minimum contract rate and variable annuities, which can be invested in a variety of investments whose market returns are not guaranteed. Annuities can be sold to individuals, or to groups through employer-sponsored retirement plans.

[6]Financial guaranty insurance covers financial loss resulting from default or insolvency, interest rate-level changes, currency exchange rate changes, restrictions imposed by foreign governments, or changes in the value of specific goods or products. According to the Association of Financial Guaranty Insurers, these companies generally provide insurance in the sectors of public finance, infrastructure finance, and asset backed securities. Mortgage guaranty insurance (otherwise known as private mortgage insurance) protects a mortgage lender if a home owner defaults on a loan. In financial and mortgage guaranty insurance, the policyholders are commercial entities rather than individual consumers.

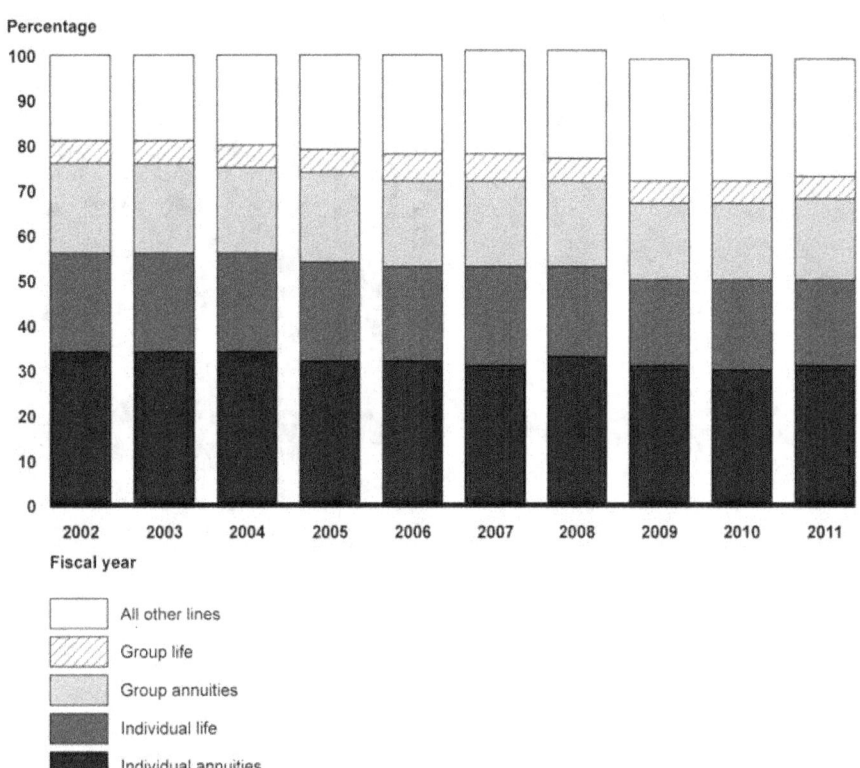

Figure 1: Premiums Written for Selected Lines of Life Insurance Business as a Percentage of Total Premiums Written, 2002-2011

Source: GAO analysis of statutory financial statement data in SNL Financial.

Note: Data for some years do not add up to 100 percent due to rounding.

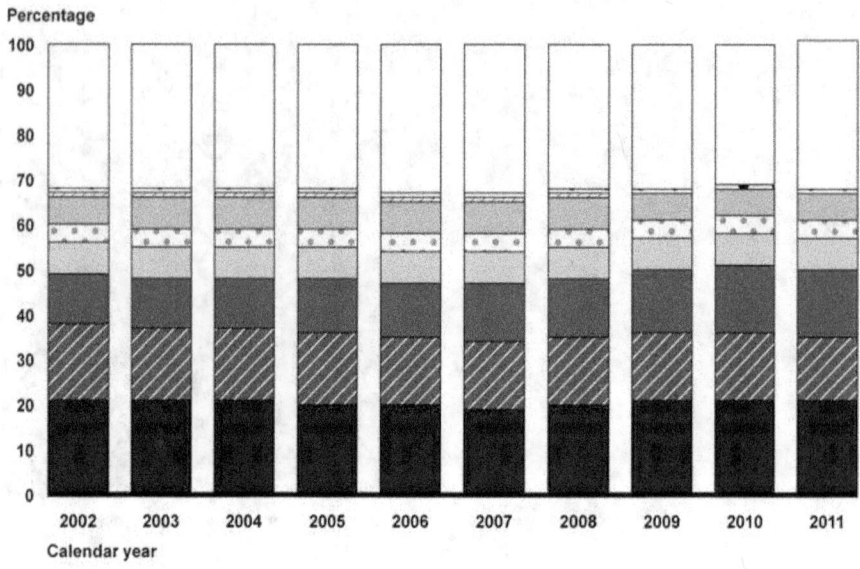

**Figure 2: Premiums Written for Selected Lines of Property/Casualty Insurance Business, as a Percentage of Total Premiums Written, 2002-2011**

Source: GAO analysis of statutory financial statement data in SNL Financial.

Note: Data for some years do not add up to 100 percent due to rounding

In general, life and P/C insurers have two primary sources of revenue: premiums (from selling insurance or annuities) and investment income. When the revenues they collect are greater than the claims and other expenses they pay, an insurer earns a profit. Both life and P/C insurers collect premiums in order to pay policyholder claims. Further, both life and P/C insurers earn investment income from unearned premium reserves, loss reserves and policyholder surplus. However, because of differences in potential claims, their investment strategies also generally differ. For instance, life insurance companies have longer-term liabilities than P/C

GAO-13-583 State-Based Insurance

insurers, so life insurance companies invest more heavily in longer-term assets, such as high-grade corporate bonds with 30-year maturities. P/C insurers, however, have shorter-term liabilities and tend to invest in a mix of lower-risk, conservative investments such as government and municipal bonds, higher-grade corporate bonds, short-term securities, and cash.

## Regulatory Overview

Insurance is regulated primarily by state insurance regulators who are responsible for enforcing state insurance laws and regulations. State regulators license agents, review insurance products and premium rates, and examine insurers' financial solvency and market conduct. State insurance regulators typically conduct on-site financial solvency examinations every 3 to 5 years, although they may do so more frequently for some insurers, and may perform additional examinations as needed. In addition to on-site monitoring, state insurance regulators, through NAIC, collect financial information from insurers for ongoing financial solvency monitoring purposes. State regulators generally carry out market conduct examinations in response to specific consumer complaints or regulatory concerns and monitor the resolution of consumer complaints against insurers.

NAIC is the voluntary association of the heads of insurance departments from the 50 states, the District of Columbia, and five U.S. territories. While NAIC does not regulate insurers, according to NAIC officials, it does provide services designed to make certain interactions between insurers and regulators more efficient. According to NAIC, these services include providing detailed insurance data to help regulators analyze insurance sales and practices; maintaining a range of databases useful to regulators; and coordinating regulatory efforts by providing guidance, model laws and regulations, and information-sharing tools. Generally, a model act or law is meant as a guide for subsequent legislation. State legislatures may adopt model acts in whole or in part, or they may modify them to fit their needs.

The Federal Insurance Office (FIO) was established by the Dodd-Frank Wall Street Reform and Consumer Protection Act (Dodd-Frank Act). Although FIO is not a regulator or supervisor, it monitors certain aspects of the insurance industry, including identifying issues or gaps in the regulation of insurers that could contribute to a systemic crisis in the insurance industry or the U.S. financial system. FIO also coordinates federal efforts and develops federal policy on international insurance matters. FIO represents the interests of the U.S. federal government in the International Association of Insurance Supervisors (IAIS), while NAIC and the states represent the interests of the insurance regulators at IAIS.[7] Additionally, some insurance companies are owned by thrift holding companies that are regulated by the Federal Reserve System.

## Risk-Based Capital Requirements and Guaranty Funds

State regulators require insurance companies to maintain specific levels of capital to continue to conduct business. NAIC's Risk-Based Capital (RBC) for Insurers Model Act applies to life and P/C insurance companies, and most U.S. insurance jurisdictions have adopted statutes, regulations, or bulletins that are substantially similar to NAIC's Model Act, as the model act is an accreditation standard at NAIC. Under this act, state insurance regulators determine the minimum amount of capital appropriate for a reporting entity (i.e., insurers) to support its overall business operations, taking into consideration its size and risk profile. It also provides the thresholds for regulatory intervention when an insurer is financially troubled. RBC limits the amount of risk a company can take and requires a company with a higher amount of risk to hold a higher amount of capital. Generally, the RBC formulas focus on risk related to (1) assets held by an insurer, (2) insurance policies written by the insurer, and (3) other risks affecting the insurer. A separate RBC formula exists for each of the primary insurance types that focus on the material risks common to that type. For instance, RBC for life insurers includes interest rate risk, because of the material risk of losses from changes in interest rate levels on the long-term investments that these insurers generally hold.

States have separate guaranty funds for life and P/C insurance to help ensure that policyholders continue to receive coverage if their insurer becomes insolvent, or unable to meet its liabilities.[8] Generally, insolvencies are funded by the remaining assets of the insolvent insurer

---

[7]The International Association of Insurance Supervisors represents insurance regulators and supervisors of more than 200 jurisdictions in nearly 140 countries. Its objectives are to promote effective and globally consistent supervision of the insurance industry in order to develop and maintain fair, safe, and stable insurance markets for the benefit and protection of policyholders; and contribute to global financial stability.

[8]Guaranty funds for life and P/C insurance are similar to the Federal Deposit Insurance Corporation for insured depository institutions. Guaranty funds pay covered claims within limits set by individual state laws and the insurance contract. For instance, the overall benefit "cap" in most states for an individual life or property casualty policy is $300,000, though some states have maximums that are higher.

and also by the guaranty funds, which are funded by assessments on insurers doing business in their state. The National Organization of Life and Health Guaranty Associations and the National Conference of Insurance Guaranty Funds represent the state life and P/C guaranty funds, respectively. Certain products, such as certain variable annuities, financial guaranty insurance, and mortgage guaranty insurance, are not covered by state guaranty funds.

## Effects of the Crisis Were Limited Largely to Certain Products and Lines of Insurance

The financial crisis generally had a limited effect on the insurance industry and policyholders, with the exception of certain annuity products in the life insurance industry and the financial and mortgage guaranty lines of insurance in the P/C industry. Several large insurers—particularly on the life side—experienced capital and liquidity pressure, but capital levels generally rebounded quickly. Historically, the number of insurance company insolvencies has been small and did not increase significantly during the crisis. Also, the effects on life and P/C insurers' investments, underwriting performance, and premium revenues were limited. However, the crisis did affect life insurers that offered variable annuities with optional guaranteed living benefits (GLB), as well as financial and mortgage guaranty insurers—a small subset of the P/C industry.[9] Finally, the crisis had a generally minor effect on policyholders, but some mortgage and financial guaranty policyholders received partial claims or faced decreased availability of coverage.

[9]A variable annuity is an insurance contract in which a consumer makes payments that are held in a separate account of the insurer. While the insurance company is the owner of the separate account assets, the assets are held for the benefit of consumers. In return, the insurer agrees to make periodic payments beginning immediately or at some future date. The consumer bears the risk of investment losses in the separate account. However, GLBs generally guarantee certain benefit amounts should the account value fall below a given level or fail to achieve certain performance levels. There are several types of GLBs, including guaranteed lifetime withdrawal benefits, guaranteed minimum income benefits, guaranteed minimum accumulation benefits, and others. GAO reviewed certain aspects of guaranteed lifetime withdrawal benefits in GAO, *Retirement Security: Annuities with Guaranteed Lifetime Withdrawals Have Both Benefits and Risks, but Regulation Varies across States,* GAO-13-75, (Washington, D.C.: Dec. 10, 2012).

# The Financial Crisis Had a Limited Effect on Most Insurers' Operations

## Insurers Experienced Some Capital and Liquidity Pressure, but Insolvencies Were Limited

Many life insurance companies experienced capital deterioration in 2008, reflecting declines in net income and increases in unrealized losses on investment assets.[10] Realized losses of $59.6 billion contributed to steep declines in life insurers' net income that year. The realized losses stemmed from other-than-temporary impairments on long-term bonds (primarily mortgage-backed securities, or MBS) and from the sale of equities whose values had recently declined.[11] A dozen large life insurance groups accounted for 77 percent of the total realized losses in 2008, with AIG alone, accounting for 45 percent of the realized losses.[12] As illustrated in figure 3, life insurers' net income decreased from 2007 to 2008, from positive income of $31.9 billion to negative income (a loss) of $52.2 billion. However, it rebounded back to positive income of $21.4 billion in 2009, largely as a result of decreased underwriting losses and expenses. Income increased further to $27.9 billion in 2010 but fell

---

[10]For assets that are sold (or impaired), realized gains/(losses) represent the appreciation or decline in the assets' value between the date of purchase and the date of sale (or impairment). For assets that are unsold, unrealized gains or losses represent appreciation or decline in the unsold assets' value. When assets are sold, their realized gain or loss is shown on the insurance company's income statement; any unrealized gain or loss is not included within the income statement. However, unrealized gains or losses are taken into account in determining the insurance company's capital.

[11]An other-than-temporary impairment is a charge taken on a security whose fair value has fallen below the carrying value on the balance sheet and its value is not expected to recover through the holding period of the security. Long-term bonds are bonds with a long maturity period—generally at least 10 or 15 years. MBS are created when originating mortgage lenders sell or assign their interest in both the note and the deed of trust to other financial institutions for the purpose of securitizing the mortgage. Through securitization, the purchasers of these mortgages then package them into pools and issue securities known as MBS for which the mortgages serve as collateral. These securities pay interest and principal to their investors, which include financial institutions, pension funds, or other institutional investors, such as insurance companies. According to NAIC, insurers claimed approximately $29.7 billion in other-than-temporary impairments on their non-agency MBS from 2008 through 2011, with more than 80 percent of that amount occurring in 2008 and 2009. However, a representative of one life insurer we interviewed noted that the values of the company's MBS holdings had recently rebounded, and a representative of another life insurer noted that they were holding onto their MBS in the hope of recovering their losses when they are eventually sold.

[12]See tables 6 and 7 in appendix II for more detail on life insurers with more than $1 billion in realized or unrealized losses in 2008 and 2009.

again—to $14.2 billion—in 2011, reflecting increased underwriting losses and expenses.

**Figure 3: Life and Property/Casualty Insurers' Net Income and Capital, 2002-2011**

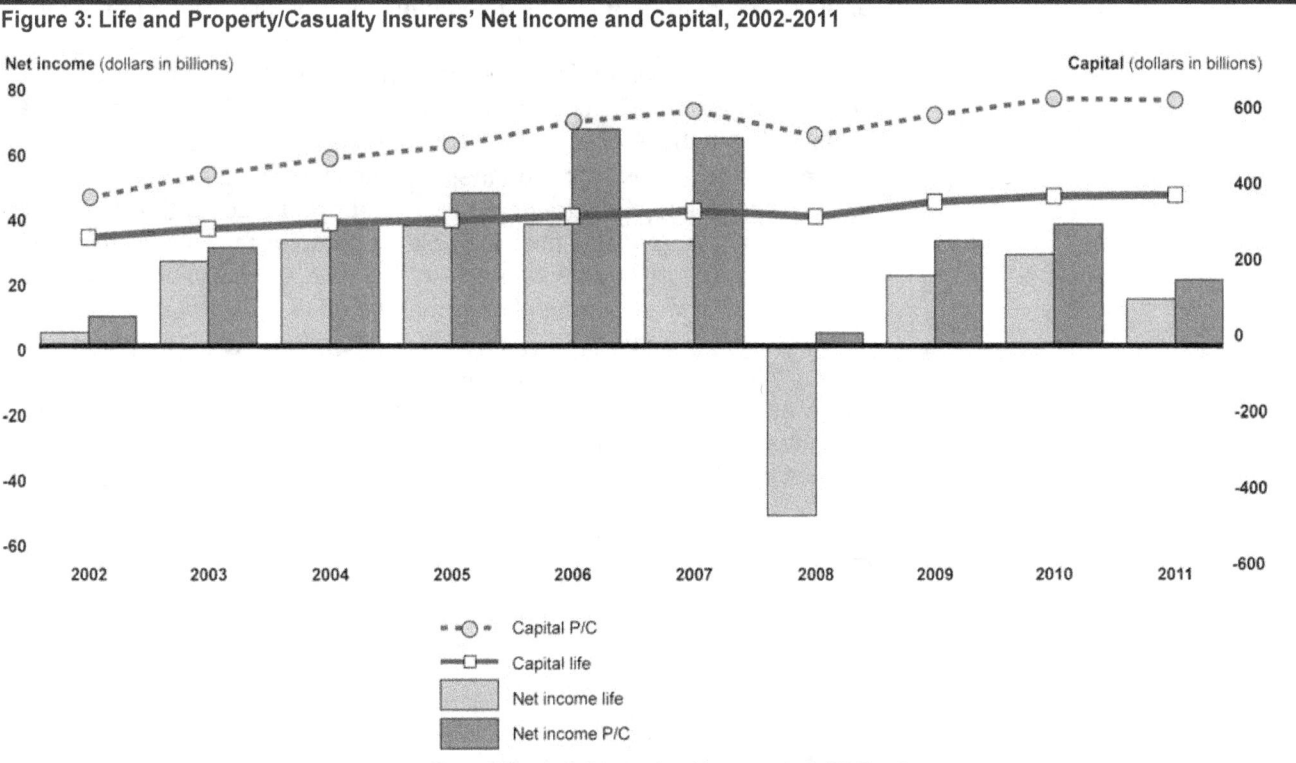

Source: GAO analysis of statutory financial statement data in SNL Financial.

Note: Data are shown in nominal dollars.

Total unrealized losses of $63.8 billion in the life insurance industry, combined with the decline in net income, contributed to a modest capital decline of 6 percent, to $253.0 billion, in 2008.[13] As with realized losses, AIG accounted for 47 percent of total unrealized losses, and seven large insurance groups accounted for another 35 percent (see app. II). The majority of the unrealized losses occurred in common stocks and other invested assets (e.g., investments in limited partnerships and joint

---

[13]Throughout this report, we use the term "capital" to mean capital and surplus for life insurers and policyholders' surplus for P/C insurers. Both measures generally refer to the excess of an insurance company's assets above its legal obligations to meet the benefits, or liabilities, payable to its policyholders.

venture entities).[14] However, the unrealized losses and declines in net income were addressed by a substantial increase in capital infusions from issuance of company stock or debt in the primary market, transfer of existing assets from the holding company, or, notably, from agreements with the U.S. Treasury or Federal Reserve (see paid in capital or surplus in fig. 4). AIG accounted for more than half (55 percent) of the capital infusions in 2008, reflecting an agreement with the U.S. Treasury for the Treasury's purchase of about $40 billion in equity.[15] Some other large life insurance companies—through their holding companies—were also able to raise needed capital through equity or debt issuance, or through the transfer of existing assets from the holding companies. As shown in figure 4, many publicly traded life insurers or their holding companies continued to pay stockholder dividends throughout the crisis. Life insurers' capital, increased by 15 percent, to $291.9 billion, from 2008 to 2009, partly as a result of the increase in net income. By 2011, life insurers had net unrealized gains of $20.8 billion, indicating improvements in the value of their investment portfolios.

---

[14]Common stock is a security representing equity ownership of a company's assets. Voting rights are normally accorded to holders of common stock.

[15]This was part of AIG's TARP assistance. See GAO, *Troubled Asset Relief Program: Status of Government Assistance Provided to AIG,* GAO-09-975, (Washington, D.C.: Sept. 21, 2009).

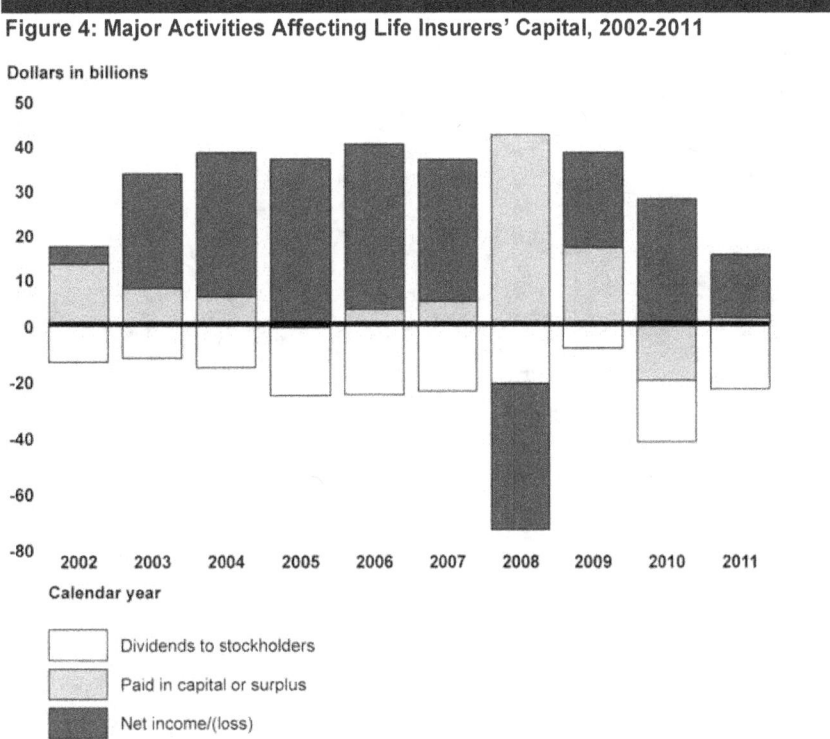

**Figure 4: Major Activities Affecting Life Insurers' Capital, 2002-2011**

Dollars in billions

Calendar year

☐ Dividends to stockholders

☐ Paid in capital or surplus

■ Net income/(loss)

Source: GAO analysis of statutory financial statement data in SNL Financial.

Notes:

Data are shown in nominal dollars.

Paid in capital and surplus, stockholder dividends, and net income are three of many factors that affect capital.

During the crisis, aggregated stock prices of publicly traded life insurers declined substantially. As figure 5 illustrates, aggregate stock prices (based on an index of 21 life insurance companies) began falling in November 2007 and had declined by a total of 79 percent by February 2009. Although prices rose starting in March 2009, they had not rebounded to pre-2008 levels by the end of 2011. In comparison, the New York Stock Exchange (NYSE) Composite Index declined by a total of 55 percent during the same time period. See appendix II for additional analysis of stock prices.

**Figure 5: Month-End Closing Stock Levels for Publicly Traded Life and Property/Casualty Companies, December 2004-December 2011**

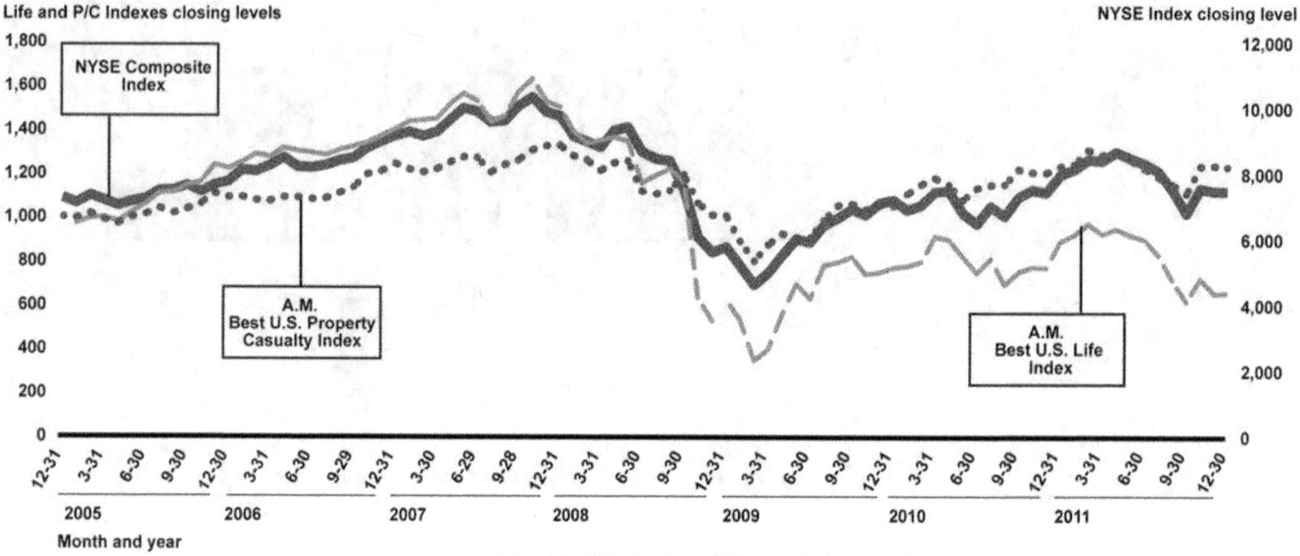

Source: GAO analysis of A.M. Best data on the A.M. Best U. S. Life and Property Casualty Indexes and the New York Stock Exchange Composite Index.

Notes:

According to A.M. Best, an insurance rating and information provider, the A.M. Best U.S. Life and Property Casualty Insurance Indexes provide a benchmark for assessing investor confidence that often correlates with general financial performance of the overall insurance industry, a specific insurance business segment, and specific companies in the context of their business segments. The indexes include all insurance industry companies that are publicly traded on major global stock exchanges that also have an A.M. Best rating, or that have an insurance subsidiary with an A.M. Best rating. They are based on the aggregation of the prices of the individual publicly traded stocks and weighted for their respective free float market capitalizations. The life index represents 21 life insurance companies and the P/C index represents 56 P/C companies. As of February 24, 2012 (the most recent date for which index composition data were available), the NYSE Composite Index represented 1,867 companies that trade on the New York Stock Exchange.

The left vertical axis represents the basis for the A.M. Best life and P/C indexes; they are based on an index value of 1,000 as of December 31, 2004, when A.M. Best established the indexes. The right vertical axis is the basis for the NYSE Composite Index, which is based on an index value of 5,000 as of December 31, 2002, when a new methodology for the index took effect. We overlaid the lines to more effectively compare changes in the indexes over time.

P/C insurers also experienced a steep decline in net income during the crisis, with a drop of 94 percent from 2007 to 2008, although the industry's net income remained positive at $3.7 billion (see previous fig. 3). Realized losses of $25.5 billion contributed to the decline in net income. Seven P/C insurance groups, including six large groups and one smaller financial guaranty insurance group, accounted for 47 percent of the realized losses in 2008.[16] The realized losses resulted primarily from other-than-temporary impairments taken on certain bonds and preferred and common stocks.[17] Net underwriting losses of $19.6 billion (compared to net underwriting gains of $21.6 billion in 2007) also affected net income for the P/C industry in 2008, as did declines in net investment income and other factors. Many of the insurers with the greatest declines in net income from 2007 to 2008 were primarily financial and mortgage guaranty companies.

P/C insurers' capital also declined from 2007 to 2008, to $466.6 billion (a 12 percent decline). Although the reduction in net income was a major factor in the capital decline, unrealized losses of $85.6 billion also played a role. The greatest unrealized losses occurred in common stocks and other invested assets. Three large P/C insurance groups accounted for 55 percent of the losses. Capital infusions mitigated the decline in capital, as illustrated in figure 6, and P/C insurers or their holding companies continued to pay stockholder dividends. P/C insurers' capital increased by 11.6 percent and 8.3 percent from the previous year, respectively, in 2009 and 2010.

---

[16]See tables 8 and 9 in appendix II for more detail on P/C insurers with more than $1 billion in realized or unrealized losses in 2008 and 2009.

[17]Preferred stocks are equities with a class of ownership in a corporation that has a higher claim on the assets and earnings than common stock. Preferred stock generally has a dividend that must be paid out before dividends to common stockholders and the shares usually do not have voting rights.

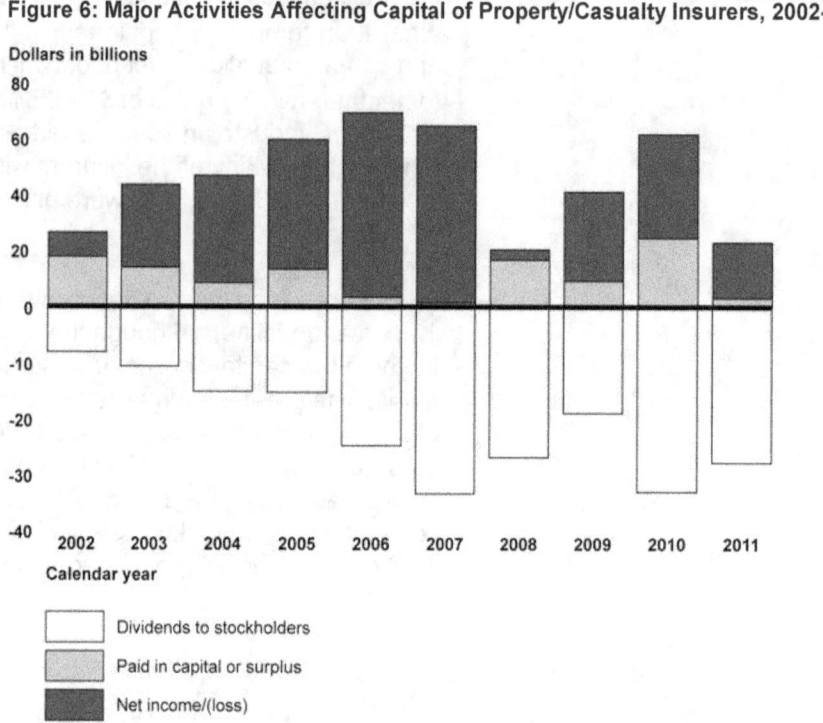

**Figure 6: Major Activities Affecting Capital of Property/Casualty Insurers, 2002-2011**

Dollars in billions

Calendar year

- Dividends to stockholders
- Paid in capital or surplus
- Net income/(loss)

Source: GAO analysis of statutory financial statement data in SNL Financial.

Notes:

Data are shown in nominal dollars.

Paid in capital and surplus, stockholder dividends, and net income are three of many factors that affect capital.

Aggregated stock prices of publicly traded P/C companies declined less severely than those of life insurance companies during the crisis. As figure 5 demonstrates, P/C companies, like life insurance companies, saw their lowest stock prices in February 2009, representing a 40 percent decline from the highest closing price in December 2007. However, prices had rebounded to 2006 levels by mid-to-late 2009 and remained there through 2011. See appendix II for additional analysis of stock prices.

While regulators we interviewed stated that most life and P/C insurers' strong capital positions just before the crisis helped minimize liquidity challenges during the crisis, many still experienced pressures on capital and liquidity. For example, a representative of the life insurance industry and a regulator noted that it was extremely challenging for most insurers—as well as banks and other financial services companies—to independently raise external capital during this time, which led to some insurers' participation in federal programs designed to enhance liquidity. In addition, some life insurers were required to hold additional capital because of rating downgrades to some of their investments. Mortgage and financial guaranty insurers with heavy exposure to mortgages and mortgage-related securities experienced liquidity issues later in the crisis, when mortgage defaults resulted in unprecedented levels of claims. In addition to maintaining the ability to pay claims, it is important for insurers to meet minimum capital standards to maintain their credit ratings, which help them attract policyholders and investors.

## The Insurance Industry Experienced Relatively Few Receiverships and Insolvencies

During this period few insurance companies failed—less than 1 percent. The number of life and P/C companies that go into receivership and liquidation tends to vary from year to year with no clear trend (see table 1). While the number of life insurers being placed into receivership peaked in 2009, receiverships and liquidations for P/C companies in 2009 were generally consistent with other years (except 2008, when incidences declined). Specifically, throughout the 10-year review period, life insurance receiverships and liquidations averaged about 6 and 4 per year, respectively. In 2009, there were 12 receiverships and 6 liquidations. P/C receiverships and liquidations averaged about 15 and 13 per year, respectively; in 2009, there were 15 receiverships and 13 liquidations. However, these companies represented a small fraction of active companies in those years. There were more than 1,100 active individual life companies and 3,000 active individual P/C companies from 2007 through 2009. Appendix II provides information on the assets and net equity (assets minus liabilities) of insurers that were liquidated from 2002 through 2011.

**Table 1: Number of Receiverships and Liquidations for Life and Property/Casualty Companies, 2002-2011**

|  |  | 2002 | 2003 | 2004 | 2005 | 2006 | 2007 | 2008 | 2009 | 2010 | 2011 |
|---|---|---|---|---|---|---|---|---|---|---|---|
| Life | Receiverships (10-year average: 6) | 11 | 4 | 8 | 4 | 3 | 4 | 6 | 12 | 4 | 2 |
|  | Liquidations (10-year average: 4) | 7 | 4 | 5 | 3 | 4 | 3 | 3 | 6 | 3 | 2 |
| P/C | Receiverships (10-year average: 15) | 24 | 19 | 16 | 10 | 17 | 15 | 4 | 15 | 17 | 15 |
|  | Liquidations (10-year average: 13) | 16 | 16 | 11 | 11 | 15 | 7 | 4 | 13 | 15 | 17 |

Source: GAO analysis of NAIC data.

Notes:

Receiverships comprise conservatorships, rehabilitations, and liquidations. An order of liquidation typically accompanies a declaration of insolvency. Although it is not possible to determine whether the order of insolvency happened in the same year as liquidation in every case, guaranty association representatives stated that liquidation date was generally a good proxy for the insolvency date.

NAIC provided data on conservatorships, rehabilitations, and liquidations that occurred during our review period of 2002 through 2011. They counted the earliest instance of one of these three conditions as a receivership for a given year. For example, a company could have gone into conservatorship in 2002 and into liquidation in 2004. In that case, it would be counted as a receivership in 2002 and as a liquidation— but not a receivership—in 2004, to avoid double counting. As a result of this methodology, liquidations reported in table 1 were not necessarily included in the total number of receiverships for the year in which they occurred.

Some regulators and insurance industry representatives we interviewed stated that receiverships and liquidations that occurred during and immediately after the financial crisis were generally not related directly to the crisis. While one regulator stated that the crisis might have exacerbated insurers' existing solvency issues, regulators said that most companies that were placed under receivership during that time had been experiencing financial issues for several years. Regulators and industry officials we interviewed noted two exceptions to this statement; both were life insurance companies that had invested heavily in Fannie Mae and Freddie Mac securities and in other troubled debt securities.[18] See appendix III for a profile of one of these companies.

## Effects on Insurers' Investment Portfolios, Underwriting Performance, and Premium Revenues Were Limited

### Investment Income

As noted above, for most insurers investment income is one of the two primary revenue streams. Insurers' net investment income declined slightly during the crisis but had rebounded by 2011.[19] In the life and P/C

---

[18]Congress established Fannie Mae and Freddie Mac in 1968 and 1989, respectively, as for-profit, shareholder-owned corporations. They share a primary mission that has been to stabilize and assist the U.S. secondary mortgage market and facilitate the flow of mortgage credit. To accomplish this goal, the enterprises issued debt and stock and used the proceeds to purchase conventional mortgages that met their underwriting standards from primary mortgage lenders such as banks or savings and loan associations (thrifts). In turn, banks and thrifts used the proceeds to originate additional mortgages. The enterprises held the mortgages in their portfolios or packaged them into MBS, which were sold to investors in the secondary mortgage market. In exchange for a fee, the enterprises guaranteed the timely payment of interest and principal on MBS that they issued. Both enterprises are required to provide assistance to the secondary mortgage markets that includes purchases of mortgages that serve low- and moderate-income families.

[19]Net investment income represents the total of all interest, dividends, and other earnings derived from an insurer's invested assets minus any associated expenses. Realized and unrealized gains and losses are also excluded from this measure.

industries in 2008 and 2009, insurers' net income from investments declined by 7 percent and 15 percent respectively from the previous year (see fig. 7). For life insurers, these declines primarily reflected declines in income on certain common and preferred stock, derivatives, cash and short term investments, and other invested assets.[20] For P/C insurers, the declines primarily reflected declines in income on U.S. government bonds, certain common stock, cash and short-term investments, and other invested assets.[21]

**Figure 7: Life and Property/Casualty Insurers' Net Investment Income, 2002-2011**

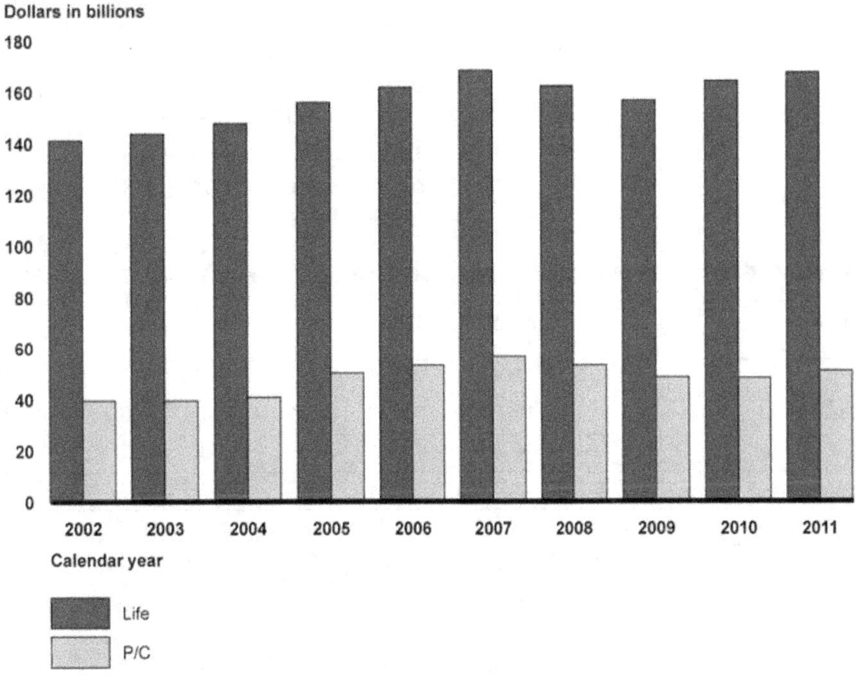

Dollars in billions

Calendar year

Life

P/C

Source: GAO analysis of statutory financial statement data in SNL Financial.

Note: Data are shown in nominal dollars.

---

[20]NAIC defines cash and short-term investments as investments whose maturities (or repurchase dates) at the time of acquisition were 1 year or less.

[21]Changes to net investment income for life and P/C insurers might also have reflected changes to their asset allocations.

Table 2 illustrates the percentages of life and P/C insurers' gross investment income derived from various types of investments. Bonds were the largest source of investment income in both industries, and they increased as a percentage of gross investment income during the crisis. Life and P/C insurers' income from other types of investments, such as contract loans, cash, and short-term investments, decreased during the crisis as a percentage of their gross investment income. According to insurance industry representatives and a regulator, going forward, low interest rates are expected to produce lower investment returns than in the past, reducing insurers' investment income and likely pressuring insurers to increase revenue from their underwriting activities. Although life and P/C companies had some exposure to MBS (including residential and commercial MBS, known respectively as RMBS and CMBS) from 2002 through 2011, as part of insurers' total bond portfolios, these securities did not present significant challenges.[22] In both industries, investments in derivatives constituted a negligible amount of exposure and investment income and were generally used to hedge other risks the insurers faced.

**Table 2: Life and Property/Casualty Insurers' Investment Income (Loss) from Real Estate, Equities, Bonds, Derivatives, and Other Investments as a Percentage of their Total Gross Investment Income, 2002-2011**

|  |  | 2002 | 2003 | 2004 | 2005 | 2006 | 2007 | 2008 | 2009 | 2010 | 2011 |
|---|---|---|---|---|---|---|---|---|---|---|---|
| Real estate | Life | 15.4% | 14.7% | 14.3% | 13.6% | 13.1% | 12.8% | 13.5% | 13.5% | 12.5% | 12.3% |
|  | P/C | 4.2% | 4.2% | 4.0% | 3.3% | 3.1% | 3.2% | 3.5% | 3.8% | 3.7% | 3.7% |
| Equities | Life | 2.8 | 2.6 | 2.8 | 3.1 | 3.4 | 4.7 | 3.6 | 2.1 | 2.2 | 2.2 |
|  | P/C | 15.3 | 14.6 | 12.8 | 12.9 | 12.8 | 12.3 | 13.3 | 12.6 | 11.8 | 12.2 |
| Bonds | Life | 73.8 | 74.3 | 74.3 | 73.5 | 72.1 | 70.6 | 73.3 | 77.7 | 76.5 | 75.7 |
|  | P/C | 72.7 | 70.1 | 71.5 | 64.3 | 66.6 | 67.0 | 71.5 | 76.5 | 74.3 | 69.8 |
| Derivatives | Life | -0.6 | -0.3 | -0.2 | -0.3 | 0.8 | 0.3 | -1.2 | -1.7 | 0.4 | 0.9 |
|  | P/C | 0.2 | 0.4 | 0.1 | 0.0 | -0.1 | 0.0 | -0.1 | -0.1 | 0.0 | 0.0 |
| All other investments[a] | Life | 8.5 | 8.7 | 8.8 | 10.1 | 10.5 | 11.6 | 10.8 | 8.3 | 8.3 | 8.9 |
|  | P/C | 7.6 | 10.7 | 11.5 | 19.4 | 17.6 | 17.4 | 11.8 | 7.2 | 10.2 | 14.3 |

Source: GAO analysis of statutory financial statement data in SNL Financial.

[22]MBS represented between 15 percent and 18 percent of life insurers' admitted assets and between 10 percent and 13 percent of P/C insurers' admitted assets during the review period. Admitted assets are assets that are permitted by state law to be included in an insurer's annual statement.

GAO-13-583 State-Based Insurance

[a]All other investments include contract loans, cash and short-term investments, other invested assets, and investment write-ins.

## Underwriting Performance

Life and P/C insurers' underwriting performance declined modestly during the crisis. In the life industry, benefits and losses that life insurers incurred in 2008 and 2009 outweighed the net premiums they wrote (see fig. 8).[23] A few large insurance groups accounted for the majority of the gap between premiums written and benefits and losses incurred during these 2 years. For example, one large life insurance group incurred $61.3 billion more in benefits and losses than it wrote in premiums in 2009.

[23]Benefits and losses refer to death, annuity, and other benefits paid out to policyholders, including surrender benefits and withdrawals (in other words, the amount insurers paid to policyholders who surrendered or took withdrawals from their life insurance policies or annuities, net of any fees charged to the policyholders within the specified surrender period). For example, a variable annuity contract with a $10,000 purchase payment may have a surrender charge of 6 percent in the first year after a purchase payment, 5 percent the next year, 4 percent the next, and so on until the charge decreases to zero. Net premiums written are the premiums registered on the books of an insurer or a reinsurer at the time a policy is issued and paid for, minus deductions for commissions and reinsurance.

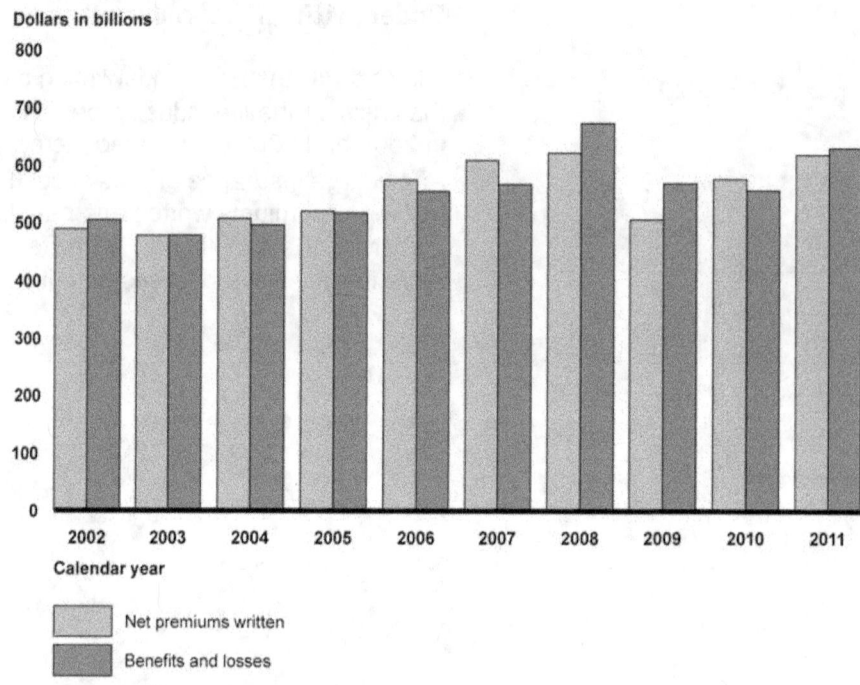

Figure 8: Life Insurers' Benefits and Losses Incurred Compared to Net Premiums Written, 2002-2011

Dollars in billions

Net premiums written

Benefits and losses

Source: GAO analysis of statutory financial statement data in SNL Financial.

Note: Data are shown in nominal dollars.

Policyholders surrendered or allowed to lapse a slightly larger percentage of life insurance policies during the crisis for both group and individual life policies, but surrender and lapse rates for individual life policies were at or below 1.2 percent and 7.4 percent, respectively, of all policies. One insurer and a regulator we interviewed stated that some policyholders cashed in or delayed paying the premiums on their life insurance policies because they needed money for other necessities during the crisis. Surrender benefits and withdrawals for annuities peaked in 2007, at $259.4 billion, following a 4 year climb. Surrender benefits and withdrawals represent the amount an insurance company pays out to a policyholder who surrenders (i.e., cashes in) or takes a withdrawal from an annuity, minus any fees charged to the policyholder. Contributing to this increase were surrender benefits and withdrawals for individual annuities, which increased 33 percent from 2005 to 2006 and another 11 percent from 2006 to 2007. By 2009, however, total surrender benefits and withdrawals for annuities had declined to $180.7 billion, their lowest level since 2004. Because interest rates dropped during the crisis, variable annuities with guarantees purchased before the crisis were "in the money," meaning that the policyholders' account values were significantly less than the promised benefits on their accounts, so the policyholders were being credited with the guaranteed minimum instead of the lower rates actually being earned. Thus, policyholders were more likely to stay in their variable annuities during the crisis because they were able to obtain higher returns than they could obtain on other financial products.

From 2007 to 2008, the P/C industry's underwriting losses increased as a percentage of their earned premiums (loss ratio), and the average combined ratio—a measure of insurer underwriting performance—rose from 95 percent to 104 percent, indicating that companies incurred more in claims and expenses than they received from premiums.[24] However, as illustrated in figure 9, the ratios during the crisis were not substantially different from those in the surrounding years. As discussed later in this report, financial and mortgage guaranty insurers' combined ratios were particularly high and contributed to the elevated overall P/C industry combined ratios from 2008 going forward. P/C insurance industry representatives we interviewed told us that the P/C market was in the midst of a "soft" period in the insurance cycle leading into the crisis. Such soft periods are generally characterized by insurers charging lower premiums in competition to gain market share. In addition, timing of certain catastrophic events in the P/C industry overlapped with crisis-related events. For example, one state regulator noted that in the same week in September 2008 that AIG's liquidity issues became publicly known, Hurricane Ike struck the Gulf Coast. According to NAIC analysis, this resulted in significant underwriting losses for many P/C insurers. NAIC determined that Hurricane Ike, as well as two other hurricanes and two tropical storms, contributed to more than half of the P/C industry's estimated $25.2 billion in catastrophic losses in 2008, which represented a threefold increase from the prior year. While the crisis may have exacerbated certain aspects of this cycle, it is difficult to determine the extent to which underwriting losses were a result of the crisis as opposed to the existing soft market or the weather events of 2008.

---

[24]The combined ratio represents the sum of the loss ratio (incurred losses plus loss adjustment expenses, divided by net premiums earned) and the expense ratio (underwriting and other expenses divided by net premiums earned). Combined ratios under 100 percent indicate an underwriting profit; ratios over 100 percent indicate underwriting losses.

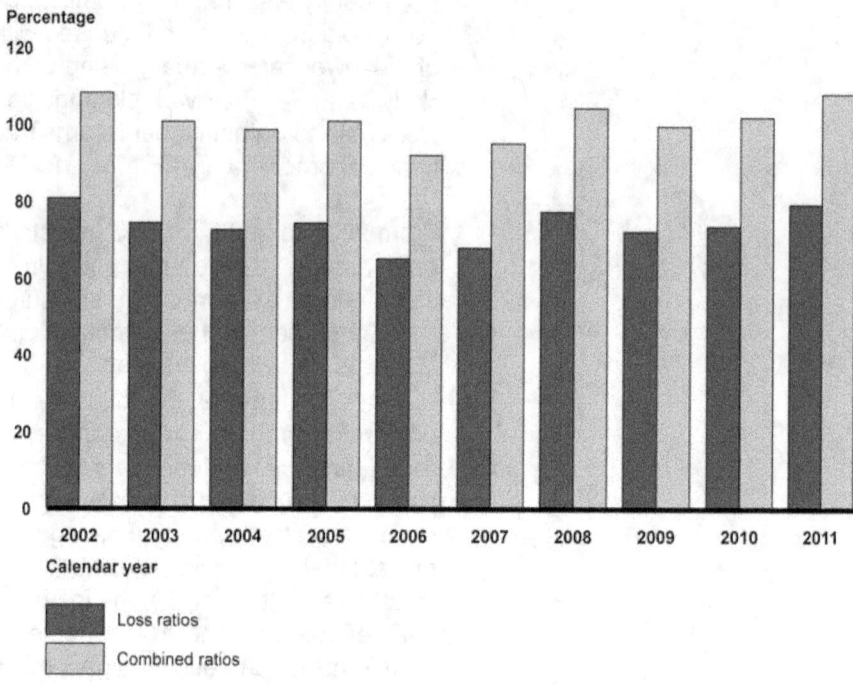

**Figure 9: Average Property/Casualty Industry Loss Ratios and Combined Ratios, 2002-2011**

Source: GAO analysis of statutory financial statement data in SNL Financial.

As noted previously, a few industry representatives and a regulator we interviewed stated that decreased investment returns may place more pressure on insurers to increase the profitability of their underwriting operations. As shown in figures 10 and 11, life and P/C insurers' net investment gains have historically outweighed their net underwriting losses.[25] As shown in figure 10, life insurers experienced net underwriting

---

[25]For P/C insurers, net investment gains/(losses) represent the sum of net investment income and net realized gains/(losses), minus capital gains taxes. Although net investment gain/(loss) is not a specific line item on life insurers' financial statements, we added the line items for net investment income, amortization of the interest maintenance reserve (adjustments to net investment income over the remaining life of investments sold, with the intention of capturing the realized gains/(losses) on those investments over time), and net realized gains/(losses) to establish a comparable measure. Similarly, for P/C insurers, net underwriting gains/(losses) generally reflect earned premiums minus total underwriting deductions (i.e., claims and other expenses incurred). For life insurers, we subtracted underwriting deductions from the sum of net premiums and other non-investment income to establish a comparable measure.

losses during every year of our review period, with the greatest losses occurring in 2008.

**Figure 10: Life Insurers' Net Investment and Underwriting Gains/(Losses), 2002-2011**

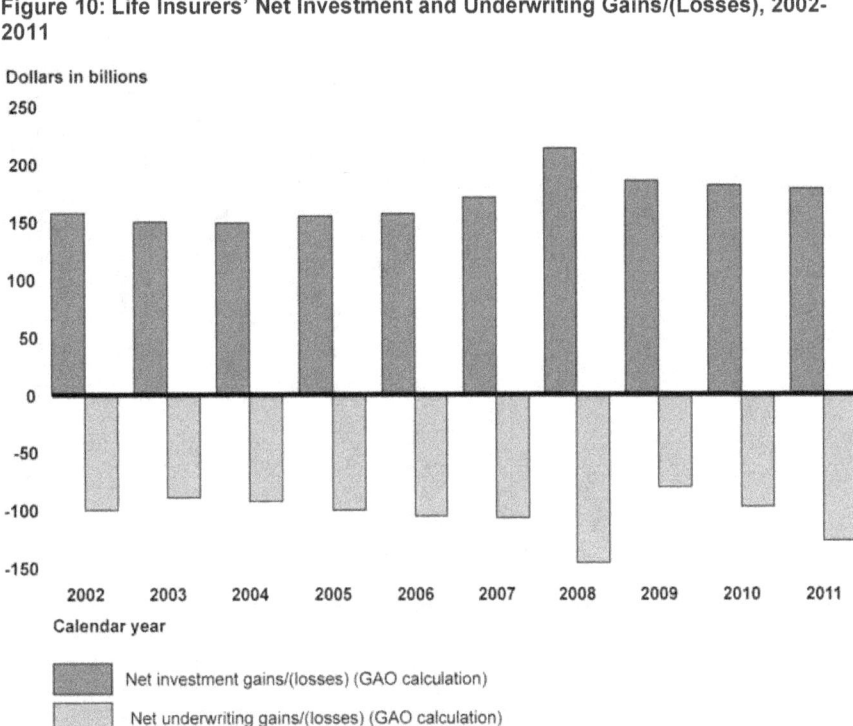

Source: GAO analysis of statutory financial statement data in SNL Financial.

Notes:

Data are shown in nominal dollars.

Unl ke NAIC's annual financial statements for P/C insurers, the statements for life insurers do not include line items for net investment gain/(loss) or net underwriting gain/(loss). We created the net investment gain/(loss) measure for life insurers by adding the line items for net investment income, amortization of the interest maintenance reserve (adjustments to net investment income over the remaining life of investments sold, with the intention of capturing the realized gains/(losses) on those investments over time), and net realized gains/(losses). We created the net underwriting gain/(loss) measure by subtracting underwriting deductions from the sum of net premiums and other non-investment income.

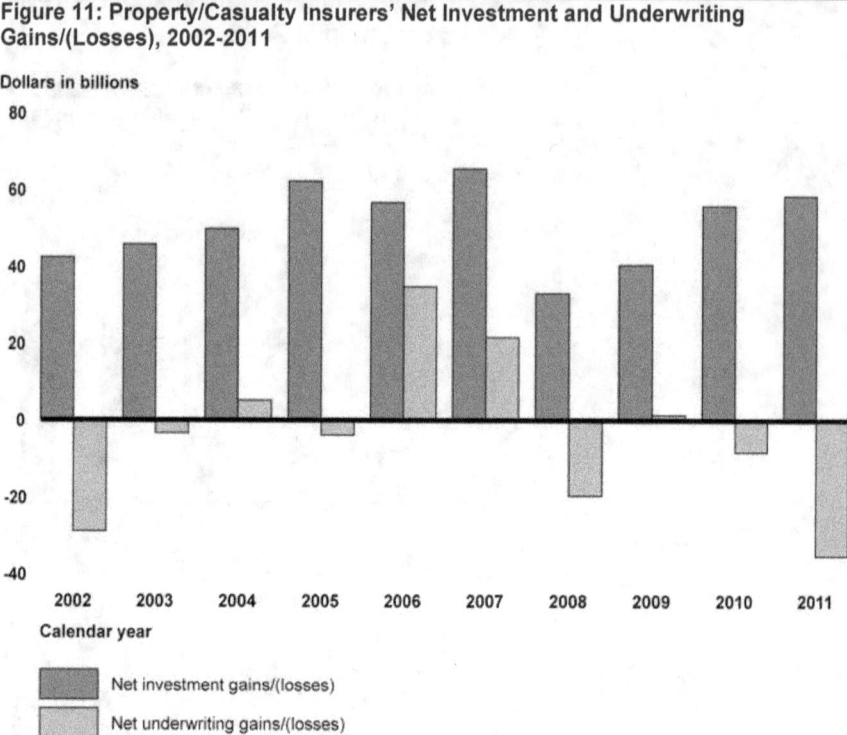

**Figure 11: Property/Casualty Insurers' Net Investment and Underwriting Gains/(Losses), 2002-2011**

Dollars in billions

Calendar year

- Net investment gains/(losses)
- Net underwriting gains/(losses)

Source: GAO analysis of statutory financial statement data in SNL Financial.

Note: Data are shown in nominal dollars.

## Premium Revenues

Effects on premium revenues were primarily confined to individual annuities in a handful of large insurers. In the life industry, net premiums written declined by 19 percent from 2008 to 2009 to $495.6 billion, reflecting decreases in all four of the lines we reviewed—group and individual life insurance and group and individual annuities—with the largest decline in individual annuities (see fig. 12).

**Figure 12: Net Premiums Written for Group and Individual Life and Annuities Products, 2002-2011**

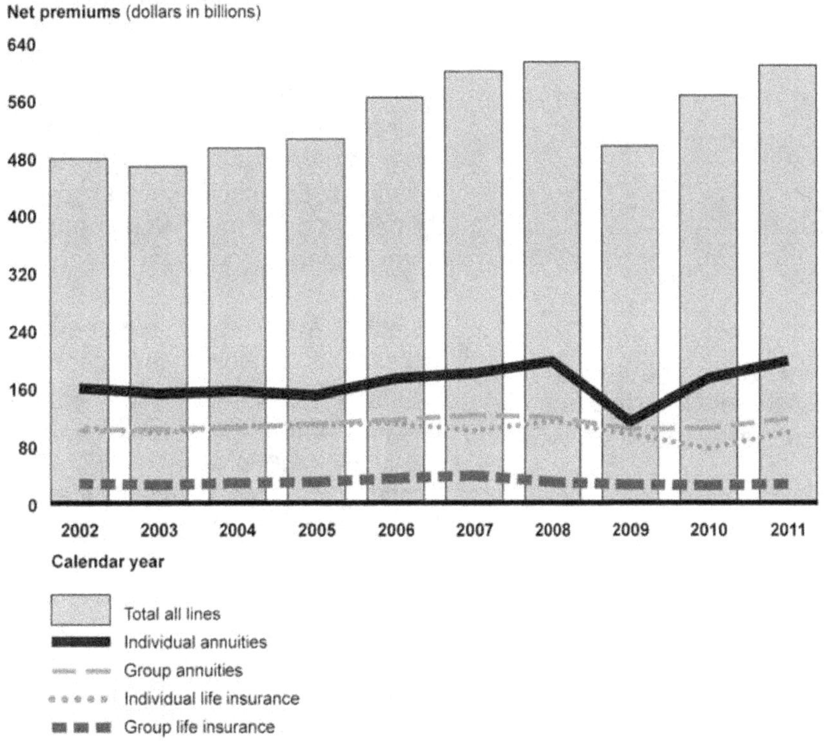

Net premiums (dollars in billions)

Source: GAO analysis of statutory financial statement data in SNL Financial.

Note: Data are shown in nominal dollars.

Individual annuity premium revenues decreased more than for other life products because these products' attractiveness to consumers is based on the guarantees insurers can provide. During the crisis, insurers offered smaller guarantees, because insurers generally base their guarantees on what they can earn on their own investments, and returns on their investments had declined. A small group of large companies contributed heavily to the decreases in this area. For example, one large life insurance group accounted for 6 percent of all individual annuity premiums in 2008 and 65 percent of the decreases in that area from 2008 to 2009. Another seven life insurance groups accounted for an additional 29 percent of individual annuity premiums and 25 percent of decreases in that area from 2008 to 2009. By 2011, net premiums in individual annuities had rebounded beyond their precrisis levels.

P/C insurers' net premiums written declined by a total of 6 percent from 2007 through 2009, primarily reflecting decreases in the commercial lines segment. In the lines we reviewed, auto lines saw a slight decline in net premiums written, but insurers actually wrote an increased amount of homeowners insurance. One insurance industry representative we interviewed stated that the recession caused many consumers to keep their old vehicles or buy used vehicles rather than buying new ones, a development that negatively affected net premiums written for auto insurance. Financial and mortgage guaranty insurers experienced respective declines of 43 percent and 14 percent in net premiums written from 2008 to 2009.

## Annuity Products and Financial and Mortgage Guaranty Lines Experienced Greater Financial Difficulties during the Crisis

As noted, many life insurers that offered variable annuities with GLBs experienced strains on their capital when the equities market declined during the crisis. Specifically, beginning in the early 2000s many life insurers began offering GLBs as optional riders on their variable annuity products. In general, these riders provided a guaranteed minimum benefit based on the amount invested, and variable annuity holders typically focused their investments on equities. From 2002 through 2007, when the stock market was performing well, insurers sold a large volume of variable annuities (for example, as table 3 shows, they sold $184 billion in 2007). As illustrated in table 3, as of 2006 (the earliest point for which data were available), most new variable annuities included GLBs. These insurers had established complex hedging programs to protect themselves from the risks associated with the GLBs. However, according to a life insurance industry representative and regulators we interviewed, when the equities market declined beginning in late 2007, meeting the GLBs' obligations negatively impacted insurers' capital levels as life insurers were required to hold additional reserves to ensure they could meet their commitments to policyholders. According to a few regulators and a life insurance industry representative we interviewed, ongoing low interest rates have recently forced some life insurers to raise prices on GLBs or lower the guarantees they will offer on new products.

**Table 3: Variable Annuity Sales and GLB Election Rates, 2002-2012**

Dollars in billions

| Year | Total variable annuity sales | New variable annuity sales | Percentage of new variable annuities sales for which GLB was available | GLB election rate for new variable annuities sales |
|------|------|------|------|------|
| 2002 | $116.6 | NA | NA | NA |
| 2003 | 129.4 | NA | NA | NA |
| 2004 | 132.9 | NA | NA | NA |
| 2005 | 136.9 | NA | NA | NA |
| 2006 | 160.4 | $116.9 | 86% | 76% |
| 2007 | 184.0 | 141.5 | 91 | 77 |
| 2008 | 155.7 | 122.0 | 91 | 83 |
| 2009 | 128.0 | 94.0 | 90 | 89 |
| 2010 | 140.5 | 107.9 | 89 | 88 |
| 2011 | 157.9 | 121.8 | 90 | 88 |
| 2012 | 147.4 | 112.3 | 85 | 88 |

Source: GAO analysis of LIMRA data.

Notes:

Data are shown in nominal dollars.

LIMRA data on new variable annuity sales and GLB availability and election rates prior to 2006 were not available (NA). LIMRA is a financial research firm that provides consulting and research services to its over 850 member financial services firms.

In the P/C industry, the financial and mortgage guaranty lines were severely affected by the collapse of the real estate market. As noted earlier, these lines represented less than 2 percent of the total P/C industry's average annual written premiums from 2002 through 2011 and are unique in that they carry a high level of exposure to mortgages and mortgage-related securities. Mortgage guaranty insurers primarily insured large volumes of individual mortgages underwritten by banks by promising to pay claims to lenders in the event of a borrower default (private mortgage insurance). Financial guaranty insurers also were involved in insuring asset-backed securities (ABS), which included RMBS. Additionally, these insurers insured collateralized debt obligations (CDO), many of which contained RMBS.[26] These insurers guaranteed

---

[26]CDOs are diversified, multiclass securities backed by pools of bonds, bank loans, or other assets. They may own corporate bonds, commercial loans, ABS, RMBS, CMBS, or emerging market debt.

continued payment of interest and principal to investors if borrowers did not pay. These credit protection products included credit default swaps.[27]

Financial and mortgage guaranty insurers we interviewed stated that prior to the crisis, these two industries operated under common assumptions about the real estate market and its risk characteristics—namely, that housing values would continue to rise, that borrowers would continue to prioritize their mortgage payments before other financial obligations, and that the housing market would not experience a nationwide collapse. As a result of these common assumptions, these insurers underwrote unprecedented levels of risk in the period preceding the crisis. For example, according to a mortgage guaranty industry association annual report, the association's members wrote $352.2 billion of new business in 2007, up from $265.7 billion in 2006. A financial guaranty industry representative told us that the industry had guaranteed about $30 billion to $40 billion in CDOs backed by ABS.

The unforeseen and unprecedented rate of defaults in the residential housing market beginning in 2007 adversely impacted underwriting performance significantly for mortgage and financial guaranty insurers. As shown in table 4, combined ratios—a measure of insurer performance— increased considerably for both industries beginning in 2008, with mortgage guaranty insurers' combined ratios peaking at 135 percent in both 2010 and 2011. In 2008 and later, several insurers in these two industries had combined ratios exceeding 200 percent.

---

[27]Financial guaranty insurers generally provided guarantees through insurance and credit default swaps (CDS). For insurance, the insurer would directly insure payment of principal and interest in the credit default event. For CDS, according to the New York state regulator, many policies sold by financial guaranty insurers into the structured finance market backed commitments by special purpose vehicles (SPV) that entered into CDS with banks and securities firms. In accordance with Article 69 of the New York Insurance Law, the SPVs, as CDS protection sellers, could offer certain contract terms that could not be legally included in policies issued directly by a financial guaranty insurer. If a credit event occurred, the SPV would be obligated to pay as counterparty. If the SPV failed to pay, the financial guaranty insurer would then be required to pay under its guarantee of the SPV counterparty obligations, even though the credit event triggering the SPV's requirement to pay may have been beyond the scope of risks that could be guaranteed by a financial guaranty insurance policy.

**Table 4: Financial and Mortgage Guaranty Insurers' Average Loss and Combined Ratios, 2002-2011**

|  |  | 2002 | 2003 | 2004 | 2005 | 2006 | 2007 | 2008 | 2009 | 2010 | 2011 |
|---|---|---|---|---|---|---|---|---|---|---|---|
| Financial Guaranty | Loss Ratio | 89% | 77% | 75% | 83% | 65% | 69% | 90% | 77% | 83% | 80% |
|  | Combined Ratio | 118% | 104% | 101% | 111% | 92% | 97% | 118% | 105% | 113% | 109% |
| Mortgage Guaranty | Loss Ratio | 84% | 72% | 79% | 88% | 68% | 82% | 102% | 105% | 110% | 103% |
|  | Combined Ratio | 110% | 96% | 103% | 112% | 93% | 103% | 123% | 123% | 135% | 135% |

Source: GAO analysis of statutory financial statement data in SNL Financial.

Note: Table 4 includes all individual companies that reported positive net written premiums in financial or mortgage guaranty insurance in any year from 2002 through 2011. We calculated the loss and combined ratios with industry totals rather than taking an average of individual company ratios.

Financial and mortgage guaranty insurers are generally required to store up contingency reserves in order to maintain their ability to pay claims in adverse economic conditions. However, during the crisis, many insurers faced challenges maintaining adequate capital as they increased reserves to pay future claims. This led to ratings downgrades across both the financial and mortgage guaranty insurance industries beginning in early 2008. For example, in January 2008, Fitch Ratings downgraded the financial strength rating of Ambac Financial Group, Inc., a financial guaranty insurer, from AAA to AA, and Standard & Poor's placed Ambac's AAA rating on a negative rating watch. Standard & Poor's downgraded the ratings of AMBAC and MBIA, Inc. (also a financial guaranty insurer) from AAA to AA in June 2008, and Fitch Ratings downgraded MGIC Investment Corp. and PMI Group, Inc.—the two largest mortgage insurers—from AA to A+ in June 2008. These downgrades had a detrimental impact on insurers' capital standing and ability to write new business. For example, because ratings reflect insurers' creditworthiness (in other words, their ability to pay claims), the value of an insurer's guaranty was a function of its credit rating. Thus when an insurer receives a credit rating downgrade, the guaranty it provides is less valuable to potential customers. Additionally, credit ratings downgrades sometimes required insurers to post additional collateral at a time when their ability to raise capital was most constrained.

According to industry representatives and insurers we interviewed, financial and mortgage guaranty insurers generally had what were believed to be sufficient levels of capital in the period leading into the crisis, but they had varying degrees of success in shoring up their capital in response to the crisis. Industry representatives and insurers also stated that early in the crisis, liquidity was generally not an issue, as insurers were invested in liquid securities and continued to receive cash flows from premium payments. However, as defaults increased and resulted in unprecedented levels of claims in 2008 and 2009, the pace and magnitude of losses over time became too much for some insurers to overcome, regardless of their ability to raise additional capital. As a result, several financial and mortgage guaranty insurers ceased writing new business, and some entered rehabilitation plans under their state regulator.[28] In addition, insurers we interviewed told us that those companies that continued to write new business engaged in fewer deals and used more conservative underwriting standards than before the crisis.

The case of one mortgage insurer we reviewed illustrated some of the challenges that financial and mortgage guaranty insurers experienced during the crisis. By mid-2008, the insurer had ceased writing new mortgage guaranty business and was only servicing the business it already had on its books. This insurer is licensed in all states and the District of Columbia. Previously, the insurer provided mortgage default protection to lenders on an individual loan basis and on pools of loans. As a result of continued losses stemming from defaults of mortgage loans—many of which were originated by lenders with reduced or no documentation verifying the borrower's income, assets, or employment—the state regulator placed the insurer into rehabilitation with a finding of insolvency. See appendix III for a more detailed profile of this distressed mortgage guaranty insurer.

## The Effect of the Crisis on Policyholders Was Generally Small

NAIC and guaranty fund officials told us that life and P/C policyholders were largely unaffected by the crisis, particularly given the low rate of insolvencies. The presence of the state guaranty funds for individual life, fixed annuities and the GLBs on variable annuities, and P/C lines meant that, for the small number of insolvencies that did occur during or shortly after the crisis, policyholders' claims were paid up to the limits under guaranty fund rules established under state law.[29] However, financial and

---

[28]Rehabilitation occurs under a court order by which a state insurance regulator is appointed rehabilitator of a financially troubled insurance company, and is given the authority to manage the company until its problems are corrected. In this situation, the regulator takes control of the insurer's books, records, and assets and assumes all powers of the insurer's directors, officers, and managers.

[29]State guaranty associations typically do not provide coverage for the investment accounts that fund variable annuities, but they cover the promises made under GLB riders on variable annuities.

mortgage guaranty insurers typically are not covered by state guaranty funds and, as described below, some policyholders' claims were not paid in full.

According to industry representatives, the crisis generally did not have a substantial effect on the level of coverage that most life and P/C insurers were able to offer or on premium rates. An insurer and industry representatives told us that due to the limited effect on most insurers' capital, the industry maintained sufficient capacity to underwrite new insurance. As described earlier, P/C industry representatives told us that the crisis years coincided with a period of high price competition in the P/C insurance industry when rates generally were stable or had decreased slightly (soft insurance market). However, P/C industry representatives indicated that separating the effects of the insurance cycle from the effects of the financial crisis on premium rates is difficult. Moreover, insurers and industry representatives for both the life and P/C industries noted that because investment returns had declined, insurers were experiencing pressure to increase underwriting profits that in some cases could result in increased premium rates.

In the annuities line, which was most affected by the crisis in the life insurance industry, effects on policyholders varied. Policyholders who had purchased variable annuities with GLBs before the crisis benefited from guaranteed returns that were higher than those generally available from other similar investments. However, as described previously, a few regulators and a life insurance industry representative told us that the prevailing low interest rates had forced some insurers to either lower the guarantees they offer on GLBs associated with variable annuities or raise prices on these types of products. According to data from LIMRA, the percentage of new variable annuity sales that offered GLB options declined from about 90 percent to 85 percent from 2011 to 2012. As a result, some consumers may have more limited retirement investment options.

Financial guaranty and mortgage guaranty policyholders were the most affected among the P/C lines of insurance, although these policyholders were institutions, not individual consumers. While most insurers have continued to pay their claims in full, some insurers have been able to pay partial claims.[30] Many financial and mortgage guaranty insurers are also no longer writing new business. This fact, combined with tightened underwriting standards and practices, may have made it more difficult for some policyholders to obtain coverage. On the other hand, industry officials have told us that the market for financial guarantees has declined because of the absence of a market for the underlying securities on which the guarantees were based; the current low-interest-rate environment; and the lowered ratings of insurers, which have reduced the value of the guarantees.

## Actions by State Regulators, Federal Programs, and Insurance Business Practices Helped Mitigate Some Effects of the Crisis

Multiple regulatory actions and other factors helped mitigate the negative effects of the financial crisis on the insurance industry. State insurance regulators and NAIC took various actions to identify potential risks, and changed the methodology for certain RBC provisions and accounting requirements to help provide capital relief for insurers. In addition, several federal programs were also made available that infused capital into certain insurance companies. Also, industry business practices and existing regulatory restrictions on insurers' investment and underwriting activities helped to limit the effects of the crisis on the insurance industry.

### State Regulators Took Actions to Identify and Address Potential Risks

During the crisis, state regulators focused their oversight efforts on identifying and addressing emerging risks. Initially, insurers did not know the extent of the problems that would emerge and their effect on the insurance industry and policyholders, according to officials from one rating agency we spoke to. Further, as the financial crisis progressed, the events that unfolded led to a high degree of uncertainty in the financial markets, they said. To identify potential risks, state regulators said they increased the frequency of information sharing among the regulators and used NAIC analysis and information to help focus their inquiries. For example, an official from one state told us that, during the crisis, state regulators formed an ad hoc advisory working group on financial guaranty

---

[30]Industry association officials told us that financial guaranty insurers across the industry are engaged in litigation against banks regarding representation and warranties made about the underlying residential mortgages that were securitized and insured. There have been some settlements with banks paying financial guaranty for some of their MBS-related losses. According to one insurer we interviewed, these and future settlements could allow companies that are paying partial claims, or no claims, to increase their payments.

insurance. The group consisted of state regulators that had oversight of at least one domestic financial guaranty insurer in their state. The group's purpose was to keep its members informed about the status of specific insurers and stay abreast of developments in the financial guaranty insurance sector. The official stated that the regulators also shared advice and details of regulatory actions they were implementing for specific financial guaranty insurers. Another state regulator increased its usual oversight activities and increased communications with companies domiciled in the state.[31]

In addition to using information from other state regulators, state insurance regulators said they also used information from NAIC to identify potential risks. Three state regulators we interviewed said they used NAIC's information to identify potential problem assets and insurers with exposure to such assets. For example, one state regulator said it used reports on RMBS and securities lending from NAIC's Capital Markets Bureau to better focus its inquiries with insurers about their risk management activities.

According to state regulators and industry representatives we spoke with, with the exception of mortgage and financial guaranty insurers, they did not identify serious risks at most insurers as a result of the crisis. A risk they did identify, although they said not many insurers were engaged in the practice, was securities lending. Two state regulators told us that to address potential risks, they created new rules covering securities lending operations. For example, one state regulator said that during the crisis it sought voluntary commitments from life insurers to limit their securities lending operations to 10 percent of their legal reserves, thereby limiting any risk associated with securities lending activities.[32] Another state regulator stated that it also enacted legislation extending to all insurers certain securities lending provisions. Both states took these actions after AIG's securities lending program was identified as one of the major sources of its liquidity problems in 2008.

---

[31]The states are principally responsible for regulating the business of insurance. An insurance company is chartered under the laws of a single state, known as its state of domicile. Insurers can conduct business in multiple states, but the regulator in the insurer's state of domicile is its primary regulator. States in which an insurer is licensed to operate, but in which it is not chartered, typically rely on the company's primary regulator in its state of domicile to oversee the insurer.

[32]The state regulator said it subsequently codified the 10 percent limit.

## NAIC Also Took Steps to Identify Potential Risks and Share Information with States

NAIC officials stated that NAIC increased its research activities to identify potential risks and facilitated information sharing with state regulators. NAIC operates through a system of working groups, task forces, and committees comprised of state regulators and staffed by NAIC officials. These groups work to identify issues, facilitate interstate communication, and propose regulatory improvements. NAIC also provides services to help state regulators—for instance, maintaining a range of databases and coordinating regulatory efforts. NAIC officials said that they identified potential risks and other trends through their regular analyses of statutory financial statement filings, which contain detailed investment data. For example, during the crisis NAIC's analysis of insurers' investment data identified companies with exposure to certain European markets that posed potential risks for the companies. NAIC passed this information along confidentially to the relevant state regulators for further monitoring. As discussed above, a state regulator we interviewed said they used NAIC's in-depth analyses to help monitor their domiciled insurers for potential risks such as RMBS. To facilitate information sharing about private mortgage insurance, NAIC officials said it formed an informal working group comprised of domestic regulators of private mortgage insurance companies. These regulators, in turn, kept other states informed about the status of private mortgage insurers. NAIC officials said this informal working group was later made permanent as the Mortgage Guaranty Insurance Working Group, which continues to assess regulations for private mortgage insurance companies for potential improvements.

NAIC officials said its Financial Analysis Working Group (FAWG), a standing working group comprised of staff from various state insurance departments, identified insurers with adverse trends linked to developing issues during the crisis and helped ensure that state regulators followed through with appropriate oversight activities. The group shares information about potentially troubled insurers and certain insurance groups, market trends, and emerging financial issues. It also works to help ensure that state regulators have taken appropriate follow-up actions. For example, NAIC officials said that FAWG analyzed each insurer's exposure to subprime mortgage assets, identified those with the most exposure, and then took steps to ensure that domestic state regulators followed up with them.[33] State regulators told us that they had used FAWG information to help identify emerging issues, potentially troubled companies, and best practices, among other things. Also, NAIC officials said that FAWG had informed state regulators about the current status of financial guaranty and private mortgage insurance companies on a regular basis as these sectors experienced more financial distress than the rest of the insurance industry during the crisis. Regulatory officials from one state said that they relied on information collected by FAWG to monitor financial guaranty and private mortgage insurers operating in their state because none of these insurers were domiciled there. They added that the private mortgage insurers doing business in their state had large exposures because of the large housing market in their state.

NAIC also expanded its Capital Markets Bureau activities during the crisis to help analyze information on the insurance industry's investments, such as exposure to potential market volatility, said NAIC officials. According to NAIC's website, the mission of the bureau is to support state insurance regulators and NAIC on matters related to the regulation of insurers' investment activities. The bureau monitors developments and trends in the financial markets that affect insurance companies, researches investment issues, and reports on those that can potentially affect insurance company investment portfolios. State regulators said they used these reports during the crisis. For example, one state said that the report on the effects of the European debt crisis on U.S. insurers was useful and another state said the reports on securities lending helped focus their dialogue with domiciled insurers about their risk management practices. As discussed later in this report, the bureau also worked with third parties to model the values of insurers' portfolios of RMBS and CMBS.

To increase transparency regarding insurers' securities lending reinvestment activities, NAIC made changes to the statutory accounting rule and added disclosure requirements to address risks that were highlighted by AIG's securities lending program, which was a major source of its liquidity problems in 2008. According to an NAIC report, AIG's problems in 2008 highlighted the lack of transparency of securities

---

[33]According to many researchers, around mid-2007, losses in the mortgage market triggered a reassessment of financial risk in other debt instruments and sparked the financial crisis.

lending collateral—specifically when the collateral was cash.[34] The report stated that the statutory accounting rule that addresses cash collateral, among other things, was subject to liberal interpretations in the insurance industry and that consequently some companies had not disclosed their cash collateral in their statutory financial statements.[35] To increase transparency, NAIC made changes to the statutory accounting rule in 2010 and subsequently replaced it with the *Statement of Statutory Accounting Principles* (SSAP) No. 103—*Accounting for Transfers and Servicing of Financial Assets and Extinguishments of Liabilities*. SSAP No. 103, which took effect on January 1, 2013, increases the details about cash collateral that companies report on statutory financial statements, such as the maturation of investments obtained with it and instances in which counterparties can call it back. NAIC also added a new reporting requirement, Schedule DL which requires insurance companies to provide more details to support the aggregate information about invested collateral reported on an insurer's statutory financial statements.

## Changes to Certain Risk-Based Capital Provisions and an Accounting Requirement Helped Reduce Pressure on Insurers' Capital

### NAIC Changed the Method of Calculating Risk-Based Capital Charges for MBS

NAIC changed the methodology it used in its guidance to state insurance regulators to determine the amount of risk-based capital (RBC) that state regulators should require insurers to hold for nonagency MBS investments.[36] As discussed earlier, life insurance companies saw a decline of almost 6 percent in capital in 2008. Prior to the change, NAIC's

---

[34]NAIC's Capital Markets, Special Report, *Securities Lending in the Insurance Industry*, July 8, 2011.

[35]The statutory accounting rule was *Statement of Statutory Accounting Principles (SSAP) No. 91R—Accounting for Transfers and Servicing of Financial Assets and Extinguishments of Liabilities*.

[36]A small percentage of nonagency RMBS were not modeled for different reasons. These nonmodeled securities included interest-only strips, foreign transactions, and some highly complex resecuritizations. For these, U.S. insurers were to continue to use agency ratings.

methodology for calculating RBC charges for nonagency MBS relied on agency ratings. For example, capital charges were lower for RMBS with a relatively high agency rating than for those with a lower rating. During the crisis, the historically high levels of failed mortgages across the nation were followed by rating agency downgrades of nonagency RMBS that required insurers to increase their capital levels. NAIC officials told us that, in hindsight, using agency ratings to help determine the amount of capital an insurer should hold for their nonagency MBS investments was not appropriate because these securities were rated too highly before the crisis and overly pessimistic after the crisis. As a result, NAIC moved to a methodology for calculating RBC charges for nonagency MBS that determined an expected recovery value for each security based on a set of economic scenarios.[37] NAIC contracts with BlackRock and PIMCO to conduct these analyses.[38] NAIC reported that this change in methodology not only had eliminated reliance on agency ratings, but also had increased regulatory involvement in determining how RBC charges were calculated for nonagency MBS. NAIC officials saw both of these results as positive.

Although this change in methodology did result in a change in RBC charges for more than half of insurers' RMBS holdings, the change did not significantly affect insurers' financial statements. Because the new methodology resulted in estimated recovery values that were higher than the amortized values of RMBS shown on financial statements, in 2010 capital requirements for 59 percent of the insurance industry's nonagency RMBS were reduced. However, almost 88 percent of industrywide CMBS holdings in 2011 were not affected by these changes. Officials from one rating agency said the change was appropriate because the new methodology was actually similar to the one used by the rating agency itself. Officials from another rating agency said that the switch to the new modeling method reduced transparency to insurers because NAIC did not release its modeling results for insurers to use until late in the year.

---

[37]NAIC changed the methodology for nonagency RMBS in 2009 and CMBS in 2010.

[38]Both firms, BlackRock and PIMCO, provide various investment services to their clients including asset management and risk management.

Some States Allowed Certain
Modifications to a Statutory
Accounting Rule on Deferred
Tax Assets

During the financial crisis, some state regulators granted some insurers permission to use prescribed and permitted accounting practices that helped the insurers improve their capital positions.[39] These practices included allowing alternative methods of calculating an insurer's assets or liabilities that differ from statutory accounting rules and can result in a higher amount of assets admitted to an insurer's statutory financial statements. Based on data from NAIC, insurers did request modifications to statutory accounting practices. From 2005 to 2007, about 30 such requests were made each year nationwide. In 2008, however, there were over 130 such requests.

For each year that an insurer has used a prescribed or permitted practice, statutory accounting rules require it to disclose in its statutory financial statements specific information about each practice it used, including the net effect on its net income and capital. For example, an insurer could request a permitted practice to use a different method of valuing its subsidiary, and a higher valuation would increase the capital reported on its statutory financial statements. Table 5 shows the net effect of prescribed and permitted practices on life and P/C insurers' net income and capital from 2006 through 2011. In 2009, the life insurance industry's aggregate net income was about $1 billion less given the effects from prescribed and permitted practices, while P/C insurers' was about $5 billion more. In terms of capital, both life and P/C insurers experienced a substantial positive impact from prescribed and permitted practices in 2008 compared to 2007; these positive effects remained through 2011.

**Table 5: Net Effects of All Prescribed and Permitted Practices on Life and Property/Casualty Insurers' Net Income and Capital, 2006-2011**

Dollars in thousands

| Year | Net effect (positive and negative) in net income | | Net effect (positive and negative) in capital | |
|---|---|---|---|---|
| | Life | P/C | Life | P/C |
| 2006 | $15,903 | $-1,256,824 | $-1,504,098 | $1,225,426 |
| 2007 | -160,886 | 530,013 | 377,626 | 6,628,204 |

[39]Prescribed practices are exceptions from NAIC statutory accounting practices that a state insurance regulator has granted or the state's regulatory provisions have extended to all companies domiciled within their state. Permitted practices are exceptions to statutory accounting practices granted by state insurance regulators to individual insurers on a case-by-case basis.

Dollars in thousands

| Year | Net effect (positive and negative) in net income | | Net effect (positive and negative) in capital | |
|---|---|---|---|---|
| | Life | P/C | Life | P/C |
| 2008 | 1,515,952 | 2,533,518 | 8,904,224 | 11,060,723 |
| 2009 | -1,014,710 | 5,242,658 | 2,048,691 | 8,192,046 |
| 2010 | 68,327 | 3,018,482 | 2,477,606 | 12,641,458 |
| 2011 | -331,882 | 167,375 | 2,658,653 | 13,611,375 |

Source: GAO analysis of statutory financial statement data in SNL Financial.

Notes:

Data are shown in nominal dollars.

Amounts represent the difference between the net income or capital reported using state prescr bed or permitted practices and what would have been reported using NAIC statutory accounting principles.

SNL Financial did not report these data on an aggregate level until 2006.

One permitted practice in particular that was sought during the crisis could generally help insurers increase the amount of admitted assets that could be included in their statement of financial position by increasing the percentage of deferred tax assets (DTA) that could be classified as an admitted asset.[40] Admitted assets are those that are available for paying policyholder obligations and are counted as capital for regulatory purposes. Statutory accounting provisions do not allow insurers to include assets in their statutory statements of financial position unless they are admitted assets.[41] Specifically, insurers requested that the limits for determining the percentage of DTAs that could be classified as admitted

---

[40]Deferred Tax Assets (DTA) record the future tax benefits that accrue each year, from differences between statutory accounting and tax accounting rules. They are used to recognize a reduction in the amount of income tax that a company is expected to owe in a future period. For example, tax accounting rules do not recognize unrealized losses of investments until they are sold, while statutory accounting rules may recognize unrealized losses before they are sold. This can make taxable income higher than statutory income, raising a company's current tax bill; but these types of differences can eventually cancel out, or reverse, in future years depending on future events, so that at some point in the future, taxable income might be less than statutory income, reducing the company's future tax bill. Statutory accounting rules determine the percentage of DTA that can be included as admitted assets on insurers' statutory balance sheets.

[41]According to the *Statement of Statutory Accounting Principles No. 4, Assets and Nonadmitted Assets,* an insurer cannot include assets in its statutory financial statement of financial position if they have an "economic value other than those which can be used to fulfill policyholder obligations, or those assets which are unavailable due to encumbrances or other third party interests."

assets be raised.[42] NAIC officials said that more than half of the 119 permitted practices that states granted to insurers in 2008 were related to increasing the limits, which in turn increased the amount of DTA that insurers could classify as admitted assets. This change enabled some insurers to improve their reported capital positions by increasing the amount of assets that were admitted to their statutory financial statements.

Industry stakeholders had mixed views on the effects of state regulators granting permitted practices on a case-by-case basis. A state regulator and an industry representative said insurance companies complained that granting case-by-case permission created an uneven playing field because some insurers were allowed to use the increased limits while others were not. However, one rating agency official said the effects were insignificant because DTAs represent a very small percentage of admitted assets. Another rating agency official added that while the case-by-case permissions might result in differences across different insurers' statutory financial statements, the financial effects of the changes were disclosed in the financial statements. Therefore, they could be easily adjusted using the disclosures to facilitate comparison of financial statements across different insurers.

## NAIC Expanded the Limits That Were Used to Calculate Admitted Assets from DTA

In 2009, NAIC issued *Income Taxes – Revised, A Temporary Replacement of SSAP No. 10* (SSAP 10R), which generally adopted the increased limits that some states had granted to individual insurers and made them available to all life and P/C insurers that met certain eligibility requirements. SSAP 10R, which superseded SSAP 10, had a sunset provision to expire at the end of 2010 and took effect for statutory financial statements filed for year-end 2009. A new feature of SSAP 10R was its eligibility requirements, which were based on certain RBC thresholds that would trigger regulatory action if they were reached. To be

---

[42]During the financial crisis, the *Statement of Statutory Accounting Principles No. 10, Income Taxes* (SSAP 10), and its revision SSAP 10R, were the effective guidance on DTAs and their potential inclusion in admitted assets. Among the limits set in SSAP 10 that insurers sought to change was a limit on how many years in the future a reversal might occur in order for a DTA to be considered an admitted asset, as well as a limit on what portion of an insurer's total statutory surplus would be used as a ceiling on the amount of DTAs that can be classified as admitted assets. The permitted practices generally allowed DTAs for inclusion in an insurer's admitted assets at a rate of up to 15 percent of statutory surplus as compared to up to 10 percent under SSAP 10, and increased the number of years into the future for the inclusion of expected DTA reversals from 1 year to 3.

eligible to apply SSAP 10R, insurers were to exceed 250 to 300 percent of these thresholds.[43] As a result, only companies at or above certain minimum capital standards were eligible to include expanded portions of DTAs in their admitted assets. NAIC officials said that troubled insurance companies that had violated the threshold for regulatory action were typically troubled and would not be eligible to include higher portions of their DTAs as admitted assets. However, they added that state insurance regulators have the authority to determine if the financial conditions of a troubled company affect the recoverability of any admitted assets, including admitted DTAs, and may disallow the company from classifying certain ones as admitted assets. On January 1, 2012, the *Statement of Statutory Accounting Principles No. 101, Income Taxes, a Replacement of SSAP No. 10R and SSAP No. 10* (SSAP 101) went into effect. It permanently superseded the original principle and generally codified the increased limits of SSAP 10R.[44] However, SSAP 101 has tiered eligibility requirements, which provide a more gradual reduction in the portion of an insurer's DTA that can be included as an insurer's admitted assets.[45] NAIC officials said that this more gradual reduction can help prevent a sudden drop in capital at a time when an insurer is already experiencing a decline in capital. That is, rather than suddenly losing the ability to count any DTAs as admitted assets, the tiered eligibility requirements can spread these reductions over time.

Based on an actuarial study, among other things, NAIC increased the limits of SSAP 10, which could provide insurers with capital relief. According to this study, one of the major contributing factors to DTAs was the large amounts of write-downs on impaired investments during the

---

[43]Specifically, the RBC level that, if reached, would trigger regulatory action is known as the authorized control level RBC (ACL RBC). Life insurers are eligible to use SSAP 10R when they exceed 250 percent of their ACL RBC; for P/C insurers, the threshold is 300 percent of their ACL RBC.

[44]SSAP 101 allows up to a possible limitation based upon 15 percent of statutory surplus and a 3 years reversal test.

[45]To be eligible for the expanded limits of SSAP 101, the risk-based capital (RBC) of a life or P/C insurer is to be greater than 300 percent of the RBC level that would trigger regulatory action. Such insurers with RBC levels of 200 to 300 percent of the level that would trigger regulatory action are to use the limits under SSAP 10; if their RBC level is below 200 percent, no additional amount from DTAs can be admitted. SSAP 101 also has separate eligibility requirements for financial guaranty and private mortgage insurance companies based upon such companies' surplus and policyholders' and contingency reserves.

crisis. As previously discussed, in 2008, life insurers had $64 billion in unrealized losses, as well as other-than-temporary impairments of $60 billion in realized losses on investments. To the extent that an insurer's DTA increased due to impairments that were taken on its investments, expanding the limits on the admittance of DTA would help to increase their capital. From 2006 to 2011, admitted DTA generally rose from over 4 percent to about 9 percent of capital for life insurers while fluctuating from about 3 percent to over 4 percent for P/C insurers (see figs. 13 and 14). The limits of SSAP 10 were intended to be conservative, explained an NAIC official, admitting far fewer years of DTAs than insurers had accumulated over the years.

**Figure 13: Admitted Deferred Tax Assets as a Percentage of Capital for the Life Insurance Industry**

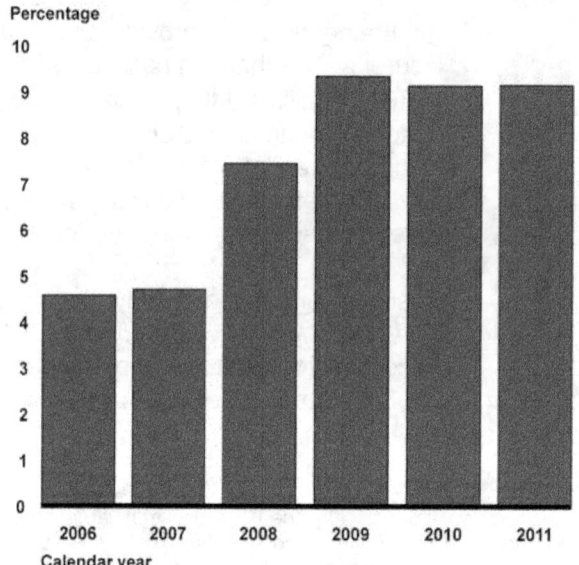

Source: GAO analysis of statutory financial statement data in SNL Financial.

GAO-13-583 State-Based Insurance

**Figure 14: Admitted Deferred Tax Assets as a Percentage of Capital for the Property/Casualty Insurance Industry**

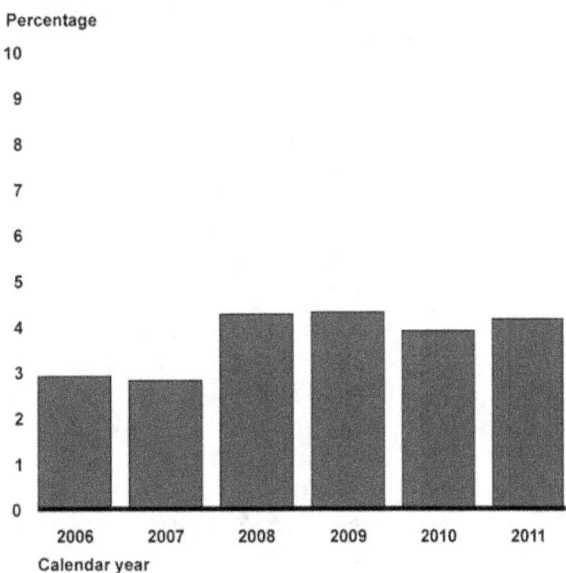

Source: GAO analysis of statutory financial statement data in SNL Financial.

Industry groups we spoke to had mixed views about expanding the limits of SSAP 10. A consumer advocacy group official stated that while expanding the limits could help insurers show greater amounts of admitted assets and capital in their statutory financial statements, in reality, no actual additional funds were made available to protect policyholders because the additional capital came from DTAs, a non-liquid asset. However, one rating agency official said the increased limits have not significantly affected insurer capital because DTAs are generally a relatively small line item on insurers' financial statements. The rating agency also said the effects of the expanded limits were insignificant and did not affect the agency's ratings, nor were they enough to make insolvent companies appear solvent. Officials from one rating agency also explained that insurers pursued the expanded DTA limits even though they were relatively small because, during the crisis, companies were not certain how long the financial crisis would last and therefore sought various avenues to help reduce stress on their capital. According to an actuarial association's report, the limits in SSAP 10R were low and therefore conservative.

## Federal Programs Have Increased Access to Capital

During the crisis, several federal programs were available to insurance companies to ease strain on capital and liquidity. Several insurers—among the largest life companies—benefited from these federal programs.

- *Troubled Asset Relief Program, the Capital Purchase Program.* The U.S. Department of the Treasury's Troubled Asset Relief Program, the Capital Purchase Program, was created in October 2008 to strengthen financial institutions' capital levels. Qualified financial institutions were eligible to receive an investment of between 1 and 3 percent of their risk-weighted assets, up to a maximum of $25 billion.[46] Eligibility was based on the applicant's overall financial strength and long-term viability. Institutions that applied were evaluated on factors including their bank examinations ratings and intended use of capital injections. The program was closed to new investments in December 2009. The Hartford Financial Services Group, Inc. and Lincoln National Corporation, holding companies that own large insurers as well as financial institutions that qualified for assistance from the Capital Purchase Program, received $3.4 billion and $950 million, respectively. A few other large insurance companies with qualifying financial institutions also applied for this assistance and were approved but then declined to participate. Both Hartford and Lincoln bought a bank or thrift in order to qualify for the federal assistance.[47]

- *Commercial Paper Funding Facility.* The Federal Reserve's Commercial Paper Funding Facility became operational in October 2008. The facility was intended to provide liquidity to the commercial paper market during the financial crisis. The facility purchased 3 month unsecured and asset-backed commercial paper from U.S. issuers of commercial paper that were organized under the laws of the United States or a political subdivision or territory, as well as those with a foreign parent. The facility expired on February 1, 2010. Ten holding companies of insurance companies participated in the facility.

---

[46]Qualifying financial institutions generally included stand-alone U.S.-controlled banks and savings associations, as well as bank holding companies and most savings and loan holding companies.

[47]Generally, companies had to be U.S.-controlled banks, savings associations, or bank and savings and loan holding companies to be eligible for Capital Purchase Program assistance. Other applicants of this program were already bank or savings and loan holding companies prior to 2008.

In 2008 and 2009, the 10 holding companies issued approximately $68.8 billion in commercial paper through the facility. AIG issued about 84 percent of this total. Of the 9 other insurance companies that participated in the facility, several became ineligible for further participation by mid-2009 because of downgrades to their credit ratings.

- *Term Auction Facility.* The Federal Reserve established the Term Auction Facility in December 2007 to meet the demands for term funding. Depository institutions in good standing that were eligible to borrow from the Federal Reserve's primary credit program were eligible to participate in the Term Auction Facility. The final auction was held in March 2010. By virtue of its role as a bank holding company, MetLife, Inc., the life industry's largest company in terms of premiums written, accessed $18.9 billion in short-term funding through the Term Auction Facility.[48]

- *Term Asset-Backed Securities Loan Facility.* The Federal Reserve created the Term Asset-Backed Securities Loan Facility to support the issuance of asset-backed securities collateralized by assets such as credit card loans and insurance premium finance loans. The facility was closed for all new loan extensions by June 2010. Prudential Financial, Inc., Lincoln National Corporation, the Teachers Insurance and Annuity Association of America (a subsidiary of TIAA-CREF), MBIA Insurance Corp. (a financial guaranty insurer subsidiary of MBIA, Inc.), and two other insurance companies borrowed over $3.6 billion in 2009 through the Term Asset-Backed Securities Loan Facility. These loans were intended to spur the issuance of asset-backed securities to enhance the consumer and commercial credit markets.

- *Federal Reserve Bank of New York's Revolving Credit Facility and Treasury's Equity Facility for AIG.* The Federal Reserve Bank of New York and Treasury made over $182 billion available to assist AIG between September 2008 and April 2009. The Revolving Credit Facility provided AIG with a revolving loan that AIG and its

---

[48]On February 14, 2013, MetLife, Inc. announced that it had received the required approvals from both the Federal Deposit Insurance Corporation and the Board of Governors of the Federal Reserve to deregister as a bank holding company. MetLife completed its sale of MetLife Bank's depository business to General Electric Capital on January 11, 2013.

subsidiaries could use to enhance their liquidity. Some federal assistance was designated for specific purposes, such as a special purpose vehicle to provide liquidity for purchasing assets such as CDOs. Other assistance, such as that available through the Treasury's Equity Facility, was available to meet the general financial needs of the parent company and its subsidiaries. Approximately $22.5 billion of the assistance was authorized to purchase RMBS from AIG's life insurance companies.[49]

A source of loans that eligible insurers have had access to, even prior to the financial crisis, is the Federal Home Loan Bank System. It can make loans, or advances, to its members, which include certain insurance companies that engaged in housing finance and community development financial institutions. The advances are secured with eligible collateral including government securities and securities backed by real estate-related assets. According to a representative of a large life insurance company we interviewed, the borrowing capacity from the Federal Home Loan Bank System was especially helpful because it provided access to capital during the crisis when other avenues to the capital markets were relatively unavailable. In other words, they were able to use their investment assets as collateral to access capital for business growth. The number of insurance company members, as well as the advances they took, increased during the crisis. In 2008, advances to insurance companies peaked at a total of $54.9 billion for 74 companies, from $28.7 billion for 52 companies in 2007.

## Insurance Business Practices, Regulatory Restrictions, and a Low Interest Rate Environment May Have Helped to Mitigate Effects of the Crisis

A variety of insurance business practices may have helped limit the effects of the crisis on most insurers' investments, underwriting performance, and premium revenues. First, insurance industry participants and two regulators we interviewed credited the industry's investment approach, as well as regulatory restrictions, for protecting most companies from severe losses during the crisis. Typically, insurance companies make investments that match the duration of their liabilities. For example, life insurers' liabilities are typically long term, so they tend to invest heavily in conservative, long-term securities (30 years). According to a life industry representative, this matching practice helped ensure that life insurers had the funds they needed to pay claims without having to

---

[49]The Federal Reserve Bank of New York created a special purpose vehicle—Maiden Lane II—to provide AIG liquidity by purchasing residential mortgage backed securities from AIG life insurance companies. The Federal Reserve Bank also provided a loan to the vehicle for the purchases.

sell a large amount of assets that may have decreased in value during the crisis. A P/C industry representative said P/C insurers, whose liabilities are generally only 6 months to a year, invest in shorter-term, highly liquid instruments and did not experience significant problems paying claims. In addition, P/C insurers' higher proportion of assets invested in equities (between about 17 to 20 percent from 2002-2011, as opposed to between about 2 to 5 percent for life insurers in the same period) helps explain their greater decline in net investment income during the crisis. Both industries also derived their largest source of investment income from bonds and these increased as a percentage of insurers' gross investment income during the crisis. Also, state regulations placed restrictions on the types of investments insurers can make. For example, one of NAIC's model investment acts, which serves as a guide for state regulations, specifies the classes of investments that insurers are authorized to make and sets limits on amounts of various grades of investments that insurers can count towards their admitted assets.

Second, industry participants we interviewed noted that the crisis generally did not trigger the types of events that life and P/C companies insure—namely, death and property damage or loss. As a result, most insurers did not experience an increase in claims that might have decreased their capital and increased their liquidity requirements. The exception, as described earlier, was mortgage guaranty and financial guaranty insurers, where defaults in the residential housing market triggered mortgage defaults that, in turn, created claims for those insurers.

Finally, low rates of return on investments during the crisis reduced insurers' investment income, and according to two insurers and two of the state regulators we interviewed, these low yields, combined with uncertainty in the equities markets, moved investors toward fixed annuities with guaranteed rates of return. In addition, industry participants and a state regulator we interviewed said that the guarantees on many annuity products provided higher returns than were available in the banking and securities markets, causing existing policyholders to hold onto their guaranteed annuity products—fixed and variable—longer than they might otherwise have done. In 2008 and 2009, the total amount paid by insurers to those surrendering both individual and group annuities declined. One industry representative we interviewed stated that, for similar reasons, policyholders also tended to hold onto life insurance policies that had cash value.

## Regulators Have Continued Efforts to Strengthen the Regulatory System since the Crisis

State regulators and NAIC efforts to strengthen the regulatory system include an increased focus on insurer risks and group holding company oversight. Industry groups we spoke to identified NAIC's Solvency Modernization Initiative (SMI) and highlighted the Own Risk and Solvency Assessment (ORSA) and the amended Insurance Holding Company System Regulatory Act as some key efforts within SMI. Although these efforts are still underway, it will likely take several years to fully implement these efforts.

### Solvency Modernization Initiative Places Increased Emphasis on Insurer Risks and Group Holding Company Oversight

Since the financial crisis, regulators have continued efforts to strengthen the insurance regulatory system through NAIC's SMI. NAIC officials told us that the financial crisis had demonstrated the need to comprehensively review the U.S. regulatory system and best practices globally. According to NAIC, SMI is a self-examination of the framework for regulating U.S. insurers' solvency and includes a review of international developments in insurance supervision, banking supervision, and international accounting standards and their potential use in U.S. insurance regulation. SMI focuses on five areas: capital requirements, governance and risk management, group supervision, statutory accounting and financial reporting, and reinsurance. The officials highlighted some key SMI efforts, such as ORSA and NAIC's amended Insurance Holding Company System Regulatory Act, which focus on insurer risks and capital sufficiency and group holding company oversight, respectively. Industry officials pointed to NAIC's SMI as a broad effort to improve the solvency regulation framework for U.S. insurers.

### Own Risk and Solvency Assessment

NAIC, state regulators and industry groups identified ORSA as one of the most important modernization efforts, because it would help minimize industry risks in the future. ORSA is an internal assessment of the risks associated with an insurer's current business plan and the sufficiency of capital resources to support those risks under normal and severe stress scenarios. According to NAIC, large- and medium-sized U.S. insurance groups and/or insurers will be required to regularly conduct an ORSA starting in 2015.[50] ORSA will require insurers to analyze all reasonably foreseeable and relevant material risks (i.e., underwriting, credit, market,

---

[50]ORSA will apply to any individual U.S. insurer that writes more than $500 million of annual direct written and assumed premium, and/or insurance groups that collectively write more than $1 billion of annual direct written and assumed premium.

operation, and liquidity risks) that could have an impact on an insurer's ability to meet its policyholder obligations. ORSA has two primary goals:

- to foster an effective level of enterprise risk management at all insurers, with each insurer identifying and quantifying its material and relevant risks, using techniques that are appropriate to the nature, scale, and complexity of these risks and that support risk and capital decisions; and

- to provide a group-level perspective on risk and capital.

In March 2012, NAIC adopted the Own Risk and Solvency Assessment Guidance Manual, which provides reporting guidance to insurers, and in September 2012 adopted the Risk Management and Own Risk and Solvency Assessment.[51] State regulators told us that some of their domestic insurers participated in an ORSA pilot in which insurers reported information on their planned business activities. NAIC officials told us that as part of the pilot, state regulators reviewed the information that insurers reported, made suggestions to improve the reporting, and helped develop next steps. According to the officials, the pilot allowed states to envision how they would use ORSA to monitor insurers. NAIC officials stated that they also received public comments on the ORSA guidance manual and were in the process of updating it to ensure greater consistency between the guidance manual and the ORSA model law. NAIC officials told us that they planned to conduct an additional pilot in the fall of 2013. The officials added that state regulators still needed to develop their regulatory guidance for reviewing ORSA.

Insurance Holding Company System Regulatory Act

Another issue that insurance industry participants identified as significant was oversight of noninsurance holding companies with insurance subsidiaries. For instance, industry groups we spoke with identified the need for greater transparency and disclosure of these entities' activities. One industry association stressed the importance of having all regulatory bodies look across the holding company structure rather than at specific holding company subsidiaries, such as insurance companies. According to NAIC, regulators reviewed lessons learned from the financial crisis—specifically issues involving AIG—and the potential impact of noninsurance operations on insurance companies in the same group. In

---

[51]States need to adopt a state version of NAIC's Risk Management and Own Risk and Solvency Assessment Model Act for the statute to be in effect within the states.

December 2010, NAIC amended the Insurance Holding Company System Regulatory Act to address the way regulators determined risk at holding companies.[52] As part of this process, between May 2009 and June 2010, NAIC held 16 public conference calls, five public meetings, and one public hearing on the Insurance Holding Company System Regulatory Act.[53] Additionally, NAIC officials told us they also share regulatory and supervisory information with federal regulators such as the Federal Reserve, including information on the amended model act revisions, at the Annual Regulatory Data Workshop.[54]

According to NAIC, the U.S. statutory holding company laws apply directly to individual insurers and indirectly to noninsurance holding companies. The revised model act includes changes to (1) communication among regulators; (2) access to and collection of information; (3) supervisory colleges; (4) enforcement measures; (5) group capital assessment; and (6) accreditation. Some specific changes include:

- expanded ability for regulators to look at any entity in an insurance holding company system that may not directly affect the holding company system but could pose reputational or financial risk to the insurer through a new Form F-Enterprise Risk Report;[55]

- enhancements to regulators' rights to access information (including books and records), especially regarding the examinations of affiliates, to better ascertain the insurer's financial condition; and

---

[52]NAIC's Insurance Holding Company System Regulatory Act (Model #440) is a model act. As mentioned earlier in this report, a model act serves as a guide for subsequent legislation. State legislatures may adopt model acts in whole or in part, or they modify them to fit their needs.

[53]NAIC, *Amendments to the Insurance Holding Company System Model Act & Model Regulation,* Powerpoint presentation, February 7, 2013.

[54]The purpose of the Annual Regulatory Data Workshop is to improve the quality of financial regulatory and supervisory data, by bringing together the full community of government financial data, and technology for shared learning and the exchange of best practices.

[55]According to NAIC, the Form F is an annual filing required of the ultimate controlling person(s) which identifies material risks within the insurance holding company system that could pose enterprise risk to the insurer or the holding company system as a whole.

GAO-13-583 State-Based Insurance

- introduction of and funding for supervisory colleges to enhance the regulators' ability to participate in the colleges and provide guidance on how to conduct, effectively contribute to, and learn from them.[56]

One state regulator stated that the revised Insurance Holding Company System Regulatory Act was expected to make group-level holding company data more transparent to state insurance regulators. Regulators also told us that the amended model act gave them greater authority to participate in supervisory colleges. U.S. state insurance regulators both participate in and convene supervisory colleges. State insurance commissioners may participate in a supervisory college with other regulators charged with supervision of such insurers or their affiliates, including other state, federal, and international regulatory agencies. For instance, the same state regulator stated that the authority allowed for international travel, with the insurers paying the costs. The act also increases the regulators' ability to maintain the confidentiality of records that they receive or share with other regulators.

According to NAIC officials, as of April 2013, 16 states have adopted the model law revisions.[57] Additionally, some state regulators we spoke to indicated that they were working with their state legislatures to introduce the revised Insurance Holding Company System Regulatory Act to their state legislatures. For instance, officials from one state regulator said that the new model act had been introduced in the state legislature in January 2013 and that adopting it would mean rewriting the state's existing holding company law. As a result, they had decided to ask for the repeal of the existing law and the adoption of the new statute for consistency.

Although the Solvency Modernization Initiative is underway, time is needed to allow states to adopt requirements. For instance, NAIC officials said that although they had completed almost all of what they saw as the key SMI initiatives, implementing all SMI activities could take 2 or 3 years. According to the officials, some decisions will be made in 2013, such as how to implement governance activities and changes related to RBC. For

---

[56]A supervisory college is a meeting of insurance regulators or supervisors where the topic of discussion is regulatory oversight of one specific insurance group that is writing significant amounts of insurance in other jurisdictions.

[57]As of April 2013, the 16 states are California, Connecticut, Georgia, Idaho, Indiana, Kansas, Kentucky, Louisiana, Maryland, Mississippi, Nebraska, Pennsylvania Rhode Island, Texas, West Virginia and Wyoming.

instance, the officials stated that they were looking to implement P/C catastrophe risk data analysis later this year and would then consider how to integrate their findings into RBC requirements. As mentioned earlier, ORSA is not expected to be operational until 2015. Also, most states have yet to adopt revisions to the Insurance Holding Company System Regulatory Act. NAIC officials told us that getting changes adopted at the state level was challenging because of the amount of time needed to get all 50 states on-board. For instance, the adoption of model laws requires state legislative change and is dependent on the frequency of state legislative meetings. The officials explained that some states legislatures meet only every 2 years, limiting the possibility of immediate legislative change. As we have previously reported, NAIC operations generally require a consensus among a large number of regulators, and NAIC seeks to obtain and consider the input of industry participants and consumer advocates. [58] Obtaining a wide range of views may create a more thoughtful, balanced regulatory approach, but working through the goals and priorities of a number of entities can result in lengthy processes and long implementation periods for regulatory improvements. As noted in our other work earlier, continued progress in a timely manner is critical to improving the efficiency and effectiveness of the insurance regulatory system.

## Views Varied on Increased Oversight Efforts

Industry officials we spoke with had favorable views of NAIC's and state regulators' efforts to strengthen the regulatory system. For example, one insurance association stated that NAIC and states had been reevaluating all regulatory tools beyond those that were related to the financial crisis. Another insurance association noted that ORSA would be a good tool to use to identify potentially at-risk companies before they developed problems. A third insurance association stated that coordination between domestic and international regulators was more robust now and actions taken are more coordinated. The officials also pointed to the work addressing supervisory colleges that involve regulatory actions by other countries that might impact domestic insurers. However, some insurance associations we spoke to voiced concerns about the increased oversight of holding companies, and some insurance associations and insurers also questioned the need for additional regulatory changes.

---

[58]GAO, *Insurance Reciprocity and Uniformity: NAIC and State Regulators Have Made Progress in Producer Licensing, Product Approval, and Market Conduct Regulation, but Challenges Remain,* GAO-09-372 (Washington, D.C.: Apr. 6, 2009).

Two insurance associations and a federal entity we spoke to were concerned with potential information gaps related to the increased oversight of holding companies. For instance, one insurance association told us that state insurance regulators do not have jurisdiction over non-insurance affiliates' activities and as a result, do not have access to information on these affiliates in order to evaluate if their activities could jeopardize the affiliated insurers. Another insurance association stated that there was a need to address holding company regulation, especially potential gaps between the federal and state regulators in their oversight roles. Some insurers also questioned the need for additional regulations and a few suggested that the regulators need to allow time for implementing recent financial reforms under the Dodd-Frank Act. One P/C insurer stated that imposing additional requirements on the entire insurance industry is not necessary especially within the P/C industry. The official explained that there needs to be greater flexibility in reporting and that the P/C industry fared well during the crisis as evident by the lack of widespread insolvencies. The official suggested that NAIC needs to re-evaluate whether the additional requirements are useful. Another financial guaranty insurer told us that no additional changes are needed in the regulatory structure or regulations for the financial guaranty industry. The officials stated that they are now dealing with federal regulators and regulatory changes related to the Dodd-Frank Act. Additionally, one insurance association stated that whether more regulatory coordination activities regarding holding companies are needed is not yet known because federal regulators have not finished implementing the recent Dodd-Frank reforms dealing with holding company oversight.

## Some Dodd-Frank Provisions That Address Financial Stability Include Insurance Oversight

While many factors likely contributed to the crisis, and the relative role of these factors is subject to debate, gaps and weaknesses in the supervision and regulation of the U.S. financial system, including the insurance industry, generally played an important role. The Dodd-Frank Act provided for a broad range of regulatory reforms intended to address financial stability and the creation of new regulatory entities that have insurance oversight responsibilities or an insurance expert's view, among other things. In our previous work, we noted that the act created the Federal Insurance Office and the Financial Stability Oversight Council.[59]

---

[59]GAO, *Financial Regulatory Reform: Financial Crisis Losses and Potential Impacts of the Dodd-Frank Act*, GAO-13-180 (Washington D.C.: Jan. 16, 2013).

The act also seeks to address systemically important financial institutions (SIFIs) and end bailouts of large, complex financial institutions.[60] The Dodd-Frank Act has not yet been fully implemented; thus, its impacts have not fully materialized.

- *Federal Insurance Office.* As mentioned earlier, the Dodd-Frank Act created the Federal Insurance Office within Treasury to, in part, monitor issues related to regulation of the insurance industry.[61] The Federal Insurance Office's responsibilities include, among other things, identifying issues or gaps in the regulation of insurers that could contribute to a systemic crisis in the insurance industry or the U.S. financial system. The Federal Insurance Office was tasked with conducting a study on how to modernize and improve the system of insurance regulation in the United States and to submit a report to Congress no later than January 21, 2010. The report is to consider, among other things, systemic risk regulation with respect to insurance, consumer protection for insurance products and practices, including gaps in state regulation, and the regulation of insurance companies and affiliates on a consolidated basis. Additionally, the Federal Insurance Office is to examine factors such as the costs and benefits of potential federal regulation of insurance across various line of insurance. As of May 2013, the Federal Insurance Office had not yet issued their report to Congress.

- *Financial Stability Oversight Council.* The council was created to identify risks to the stability of the U.S. financial system, including those that might be created by insurance companies.[62] The council includes some representation with insurance expertise. Some authorities given to the Financial Stability Oversight Council allow it to

---

[60]While the Dodd-Frank Act does not use the term "systemically important financial institution," this term is commonly used by academics and other experts to refer to bank holding companies with $50 billion or more in total consolidated assets and nonbank financial companies designated by the Financial Stability Oversight Council for Federal Reserve supervision and enhanced prudential standards.

[61]31 U.S.C. §313.

[62]The provisions of the Dodd-Frank Act dealing with FSOC are contained primarily in subtitle A of title I, §§ 111-123, codified at 12 U.S.C. §§ 5321-5333. And title VIII, codified at 12 U.S.C. §§ 5461-5472.

- collect information from certain state and federal agencies regulating across the financial system so that regulators will be better prepared to address emerging threats;

- recommend strict standards for the large, interconnected bank holding companies and nonbank financial companies designated for enhanced supervision; and

- facilitate information sharing and coordination among the member agencies to eliminate gaps in the regulatory structure.

Additionally, the act provides that the Financial Stability Oversight Council have 10 voting and 5 nonvoting members. The 10 voting members provide a federal regulatory perspective, including an independent insurance expert's view. The 5 nonvoting members offer different insights as state-level representatives from bank, securities, and insurance regulators or as the directors of some new offices within Treasury—Office of Financial Research and the Federal Insurance Office—that were established by the act. The Dodd-Frank Act requires that the council meet at least once a quarter.[63] One industry association we spoke to stated that Financial Stability Oversight Council members provided benefits—for instance, they were able to discuss activities that could be concerns in future crises and make recommendations to the primary regulators.

- *Bureau of Consumer Financial Protection (known as CFPB)*. The Dodd-Frank Act established CFPB as an independent bureau within the Federal Reserve System and provided it with rulemaking, enforcement, supervisory, and other powers over many consumer financial products and services and many of the entities that sell them. CFPB does not have authority over most insurance activities or most activities conducted by firms regulated by SEC or CFTC. However, certain consumer financial protection functions from seven existing federal agencies were transferred to CFPB.[64] Consumer financial products and services over which CFPB has primary authority include

---

[63]GAO, *Financial Stability: New Council and Research Office Should Strengthen the Accountability and Transparency of Their Decisions*, GAO-12-886 (Washington D.C.: Sept. 11, 2012).

[64]These agencies included the Federal Reserve, Federal Deposit Insurance Corporation, the Federal Trade Commission, the Department of Housing and Urban Development, the National Credit Union Administration, Office of the Comptroller of the Currency, and Office of Thrift Supervision.

deposit taking, mortgages, credit cards and other extensions of credit, loan servicing, and debt collection. CFPB is authorized to supervise certain nonbank financial companies and large banks and credit unions with over $10 billion in assets and their affiliates for consumer protection purposes.

The financial crisis also revealed weaknesses in the existing regulatory framework for overseeing large, interconnected, and highly leveraged financial institutions and their potential impacts on the financial system and the broader economy in the event of failure. The Dodd-Frank Act requires the Board of Governors of the Federal Reserve System (Reserve Board) to supervise and develop enhanced capital and other prudential standards for these large, interconnected financial institutions, which include bank holding companies with $50 billion or more in consolidated assets and any nonbank financial company that the Financial Stability Oversight Council designates.[65] The act requires the enhanced prudential standards to be more stringent than standards applicable to other bank holding companies and financial firms that do not present similar risks to U.S. financial stability. The act further allows the enhanced prudential standards to be more stringent than standards applicable to other bank holding companies and financial firms that do not present similar risks to U.S. financial stability. In April 2013, the Federal Reserve issued a final rule that establishes the requirements for determining when an entity is "predominantly engaged in financial activities." Among the criteria is whether an institution is primarily engaged in financial activities, which can include insurance underwriting. As of May 2013, the Financial Stability Oversight Council had yet to publicly make any such designations.

## Agency Comments

We provided a draft of this report to NAIC for their review and comment. NAIC provided technical comments which we have incorporated, as appropriate.

As agreed with your offices, unless you publicly announce the contents of this report earlier, we plan no further distribution until 30 days from the report date. At that time, we will send copies to the Chief Executive Officer of the National Association of Insurance Commissioners. In

---

[65]Dodd-Frank Act, § 165, 124 Stat. at 1423–1432, *codified at* 12 U.S.C. § 5365.

addition, the report will be made available at no charge on the GAO website at http://www.gao.gov.

If you or your staffs have any questions regarding this report, please contact me at (202) 512-8678 or cackleya@gao.gov. Contact points for our Offices of Congressional Relations and Public Affairs may be found on the last page of this report. GAO staff that made major contributions to this report are listed in appendix IV.

Alicia Puente Cackley
Director, Financial Markets
   and Community Investment

# Appendix I: Objectives, Scope, and Methodology

This report examines (1) what is known about how the insurance industry and policyholders were affected by the financial crisis, (2) the factors that affected the impact of the crisis on insurers and policyholders, and (3) the types of regulatory actions that have been taken since the crisis to help prevent or mitigate potential negative effects of future economic downturns on insurance companies and their policyholders.

To address these objectives, we reviewed relevant laws and regulations on solvency oversight such as the Dodd-Frank Wall Street Reform and Consumer Protection Act and financial institution holding company supervision such as the model Insurance Holding Company System Regulatory Act. We conducted a literature search using ProQuest, EconLit, and PolicyFile and reviewed relevant literature and past reports on the financial crisis and the insurance industry, the general condition of the U.S. economy in 2008, and the events surrounding the federal rescue of American International Group, Inc. (AIG). We interviewed officials from selected state insurance departments, the Federal Insurance Office, the National Association of Insurance Commissioners (NAIC), the National Conference of Insurance Legislators, insurance associations, insurance companies, credit rating agencies, and consumer advocacy groups. We interviewed or received written responses to our questions from insurance regulators in seven states—California, Illinois, Iowa, Maryland, New York, Texas, and Virginia. We used an illustrative sampling strategy to select states based on the states' geographic diversity, number of domiciled insurers, and premium volumes, which ranged from small (Iowa) to large (California). We interviewed regulators from six of the states and received written responses to our questions from one of the states. We also met with six industry associations representing insurance companies covering life and property/casualty (P/C), including financial guaranty and mortgage insurance; two associations representing agents and brokers; and two national insurance guaranty fund associations. Additionally, we met with six insurers covering life and P/C insurance lines, including mortgage insurance and financial guaranty insurance. The insurers represent different states of domicile and varying market shares in net premiums written. Finally, we met with two credit rating agencies and two consumer advocacy groups to obtain their perspective on how the financial crisis impacted the insurance industry and policyholders. We also reviewed congressional testimony and other documents from industry participants, several of whom we interviewed for this study.

## Determining the Effect of Crisis on Insurance Companies and Policyholders

To address how the financial crisis affected the insurance industry and policyholders, we reviewed academic papers and government reports, and interviewed industry representatives, regulatory officials, and internal stakeholders to identify the key characteristics associated with the financial crisis. This resulted in a list of five commonly identified major characteristics of the crisis, which are declines in real estate values, declines in equities values, lowered interest rates, increased mortgage default rates, and changes in policyholder behavior. We reviewed industry documents—including NAIC's annual analyses of the life and P/C industries—to identify commonly used financial measures for insurance companies.[1] These measures help demonstrate insurers' financial health in a number of areas including investment performance, underwriting performance, capital adequacy, and profitability.

We selected specific lines of insurance within the life and P/C industries for our analyses on net premiums written. In the life industry, we focused on individual annuities, individual life insurance, group annuities, and group life insurance. These lines accounted for 77 percent of average life insurance premiums during our review period of 2002 through 2011, and the policyholders were individual consumers (either independently or through their workplaces). In the P/C industry, we focused on private passenger auto liability, auto physical damage, home owners multiple peril, commercial multiple peril, other liability (occurrence), other liability (claims-made), financial guaranty, and mortgage guaranty insurance. These lines of insurance accounted for 68 percent of average P/C insurance premiums over our 10-year review period and involved individual and commercial policyholders. We chose to review financial and mortgage guaranty insurance despite their small percentage of premiums (less than 2 percent of average P/C premiums from 2002 through 2011) because we had learned through research and preliminary interviews that they were more heavily affected by the crisis. We obtained input on the data analysis plan from NAIC and a large rating agency and incorporated their suggestions where appropriate.

We obtained the financial data from insurers' annual statutory financial statements, which insurance companies must submit to NAIC after the

---

[1]Our selected measures included gross and net investment income, total invested assets, capital and paid in surplus, net cash from financing and miscellaneous sources, net income, capital and surplus and policyholders' surplus ("capital"), net premiums written, surrenders, lapses, and other measures.

close of each calendar year. We gathered the data for all life and P/C
insurers for the period January 2002 through 2011 using SNL Financial, a
private financial database that contains publicly filed regulatory and
financial reports. We chose the 10-year time period in order to obtain
context for our findings around the period of 2007 through 2009, which is
generally regarded as the duration of the financial crisis.

We analyzed data for both operating and acquired or nonoperating
companies to help ensure that we captured information on all companies
that were operating at some point during the 10-year period. The
population of operating and acquired or nonoperating life insurance
companies from 2002 through 2011 was 937, while the population of
operating and acquired or nonoperating P/C companies from 2002
through 2011 was 1,917. We conducted most of our analyses at the SNL
group and unaffiliated companies level, meaning that data for companies
that are associated with a larger holding company were aggregated,
adjusted to prevent double counting, and presented at the group level.
We also ran a few selected analyses (such as our analysis of permitted
and prescribed practices) at the individual company level to obtain detail
about specific operating companies within a holding company structure.

To analyze the number and financial condition of insurers that went into
receivership during the 10-year review period, we obtained data that
NAIC staff compiled from NAIC's Global Receivership Information
Database. The data included conservation, rehabilitation, and liquidation
dates, as well as assets, liabilities, and net equity (the difference between
assets and liabilities) generally from the time of the receivership action,
among other data items.[2] Our analysis of numbers of receiverships and
liquidations included 58 life insurers and 152 P/C insurers. The NAIC staff
that compiled the data told us that data on assets, liabilities, and net
equity were not always available in either of their data systems. To
address this problem of missing data, NAIC staff pulled data when
available from the last financial statement before the company was
placed into receivership or the first available financial statement

---

[2]NAIC counted the earliest instance of conservatorship, rehabilitation, or liquidation within
the 2002-2011 period as a receivership for a given year. For example, a company could
have gone into conservatorship in 2002 and into liquidation in 2004. In that case, it would
be counted as a receivership in 2002, but not in 2004, to avoid double counting. As a
result of this methodology, liquidations we reported in table 1 were not necessarily
included in the total number of receiverships for the year in which they occurred.

immediately after being placed into receivership and replaced the missing data. This was the case for 5 of 58 life insurance companies and 27 of 152 P/C companies.[3] We believe these asset, liability, and net equity levels would have changed little in the time between liquidation and when the financial statements were prepared, and we determined that the time difference was likely to have little effect on our estimate of the general size and net equity levels of insurers at liquidation. However, the average assets and average net equity we report might be slightly higher or lower than was actually the case for each year. In addition, out of the 40 life insurers and 125 P/C insurers that went into liquidation from 2002 through 2011, NAIC staff could not provide asset data for 7 life insurers and 19 P/C insurers, and they could not provide net equity data for 8 life insurers and 29 P/C insurers. We excluded these companies from our analyses and indicated in tables 10 and 11 (app. II) when data were not available. Our analysis of assets at liquidation included 33 life insurers and 106 P/C insurers, and our analysis of net equity at liquidation included 32 life insurers and 96 P/C insurers.

To describe how publicly traded life and P/C insurers' stock prices changed during the crisis, we obtained daily closing price data for A.M. Best's U.S. Life Insurance Index (AMBUL) and U.S. Property Casualty Insurance Index (AMBUPC). The indexes include all U.S. insurance industry companies that are publicly traded on major global stock exchanges and that also have an interactive A.M. Best rating, or that have an insurance subsidiary with an interactive A.M. Best Rating. The AMBUL index reflects 21 life insurance companies and the AMBUPC index reflects 56 P/C companies. We compared the mean monthly closing price for each index to the closing price for the last day of the month and determined that they were generally similar, so we reported the latter measure. Because 48 of the 77 life and P/C companies in the A.M. Best indexes trade on the New York Stock Exchange (NYSE), we also analyzed closing stock prices from the NYSE Composite Index (NYA), obtained from Yahoo! Finance, to provide context on the overall equities market. NYA reflects all common stocks listed on NYSE, (1,867

---

[3]The time difference between the date of liquidation and the year from which NAIC was able to obtain data in these cases ranged from about 1 to 14 years for life insurance companies and from about 1 to 8 years for P/C companies, but the average time difference was about 6 years for life insurance companies and about 4 years for P/C companies.

companies).[4] For all indexes, we analyzed the time period December 2004 through December 2011 because A.M. Best did not have data prior to December 2004.

To select the two distressed insurers that we profiled in appendix III, we focused on life and P/C companies that were placed in receivership during the crisis. Based on interviews with regulators and industry officials, we learned that the effects of the financial crisis were limited largely to certain annuity products (provided by life insurers) and the financial and mortgage guaranty lines of insurance. Therefore, through our interviews with industry associations and state regulators, we selected one life insurer and one mortgage guaranty insurer that were directly affected by the crisis to illustrate the effects of the crisis at the company level. We obtained financial data through SNL Financial and publicly available court documents to examine these insurers' cases.

We determined that the financial information used in this report—including statutory financial data from SNL Financial, stock price data from A.M. Best, receivership and permitted practices data from NAIC, and annuity sales and GLB data from LIMRA—was sufficiently reliable to assess the effects of the crisis on the insurance industry. To assess reliability, we compared data reported in individual companies' annual financial statements for a given year to that reported in SNL Financial. We also aggregated the individual company data for net premiums for two SNL groups (one life and one P/C group) to verify that our results matched SNL's, because intercompany transactions would be rare in this field.[5] In addition, we compared the results of our analysis of key measures—such as net income, capital, net investment income, and surrender benefits and withdrawals—to NAIC's annual industry commentaries and found that they were generally similar. We also obtained information from A.M. Best, NAIC, and LIMRA staff about their internal controls and procedures for collecting their respective stock price, receivership, and annuities data.

---

[4]NYA had 1,867 component companies as of February 24, 2012.

[5]We have assessed the reliability of SNL Financial data as part of previous studies related to banking and finance and found the data to be reliable for the purposes of our review. Because we had not used SNL Financial's insurance data in the past, we took additional measures to ensure their reliability.

## Factors That Affected the Impact of the Crisis on Insurers and Policyholders

To address the factors that helped mitigate the effect of the crisis, we reviewed NAIC's model investment act, industry reports, and credit rating agency reports to identify such factors. We also interviewed state insurance regulators, insurance company associations, insurance companies, and credit rating agencies to obtain their insights on the mitigating effects of industry investment and underwriting practices, regulatory restrictions, and effects of the crisis on policyholder behavior. We also reviewed our prior work and other sources to identify federal programs that were available to insurance companies to increase access to capital, including the Troubled Asset Relief Program, the Board of Governors of the Federal Reserve System's and Federal Reserve Banks' (Federal Reserve) liquidity programs, and the Federal Home Loan Bank System, including assistance to help some of the largest life insurers such as AIG during the crisis.

## Regulatory Actions That Have Been Taken to Protect Insurers and Policyholders

To assess the state insurance regulatory response system in protecting insurers and policyholders and the types of insurance regulatory actions taken during and following the crisis, we reviewed and analyzed relevant state guidance. This included NAIC documents such as Capital Markets Bureau reports, statutory accounting rules such as the Statements of Statutory Accounting Principles, and information on securities lending and permitted practices. We also reviewed the Solvency Modernization Initiative, including associated guidance manuals and model laws such as the Insurance Holding Company System Regulatory Act. In addition, we analyzed SNL Financial data and reviewed reports on deferred tax assets, including actuary association reports, a consumer group's public comments, and information from state insurance regulator and industry consultant websites. We interviewed officials from state regulators, NAIC, FIO, industry associations, insurers, and others to obtain their perspectives on state regulatory actions taken in response to the crisis and impacts on insurers and policyholders and efforts to help mitigate potential negative effects of future economic downturns. Additionally, we reviewed past reports on the provisions of the Dodd-Frank Act and the impacts on the insurance industry with regard to oversight responsibilities.

We conducted this performance audit from June 2012 to June 2013 in accordance with generally accepted government auditing standards. Those standards require that we plan and perform the audit to obtain sufficient, appropriate evidence to provide a reasonable basis for our findings and conclusions based on our audit objectives. We believe that the evidence obtained provides a reasonable basis for our findings and conclusions based on our audit objectives.

# Appendix II: Additional Data on Life and P/C Industry Financial Performance, 2002-2011

This appendix provides some additional data on life and P/C insurers' financial performance, including realized and unrealized losses, financing cash flow, P/C premium revenues, assets and net equity of companies in liquidation, and stock price data.

## Realized and Unrealized Losses

In 2008 and 2009, a small number of large insurance groups generally comprised the majority of realized and unrealized losses in the life and P/C industries.[1] Tables 6 and 7 lists the life insurers with realized or unrealized losses exceeding $1 billion in 2008 and 2009, and tables 8 and 9 list the same data for P/C insurers. All of the insurers listed are either life or P/C "groups" in the SNL Financial database, meaning that they include all of the U.S. insurance companies in either the life or P/C industry within the same corporate hierarchy.

**Table 6: Life Insurers with $1 Billion or More in Realized Losses, 2008 and 2009**

Dollars in thousands

| Insurer | Realized losses | Percentage of all realized losses |
|---|---|---|
| **2008** | | |
| American International Group | $-27,032,295 | 45.3% |
| TIAA-CREF | -4,562,314 | 7.6 |
| MetLife Inc. | -2,107,802 | 3.5 |
| New York Life Insurance Group | -1,828,390 | 3.1 |
| CNO Financial Group Inc. | -1,767,840 | 3.0 |
| Northwestern Mutual Life Insurance Company | -1,519,738 | 2.5 |
| Prudential Financial Inc. | -1,377,951 | 2.3 |
| Allstate Corporation | -1,175,618 | 2.0 |
| Allianz Group | -1,142,726 | 1.9 |
| ING Groep N.V. | -1,098,560 | 1.8 |
| Massachusetts Mutual Life Insurance Company | -1,092,727 | 1.8 |
| Lincoln National Corporation | -1,053,231 | 1.8 |
| **2009** | | |
| TIAA-CREF | $-3,451,216 | 10.6% |

[1]Realized gains/(losses) are increases or decreases in capital assets (such as stocks and bonds) between the date of purchase and the date of sale or impairment. Unrealized gains or losses represent appreciation or decline in the unsold assets' value.

Dollars in thousands

| Insurer | Realized losses | Percentage of all realized losses |
|---|---|---|
| ING Groep N.V. | -3,373,625 | 10.3 |
| American International Group | -2,864,587 | 8.8 |
| Hartford Financial Services | -2,192,781 | 6.7 |
| MetLife Inc. | -1,985,188 | 6.1 |
| Jackson National Life Group | -1,679,803 | 5.1 |
| AEGON NV | -1,644,108 | 5.0 |
| Prudential Financial Inc. | -1,544,248 | 4.7 |
| AXA | -1,391,188 | 4.3 |
| Genworth Financial Inc. | -1,057,640 | 3.2 |
| Allstate Corporation | -1,056,030 | 3.2 |

Source: GAO analysis of statutory financial statement data in SNL Financial.
Note: Data are shown in nominal dollars.

**Table 7: Life Insurers with $1 Billion or More in Unrealized Losses, 2008 and 2009**

Dollars in thousands

| Insurer | Unrealized losses | Percentage of all unrealized losses |
|---|---|---|
| **2008** | | |
| American International Group | $-30,189,534 | 47.33% |
| MetLife, Inc. | -5,002,128 | 7.84 |
| AXA | -4,931,978 | 7.73 |
| Northwestern Mutual Life Insurance Company | -4,368,554 | 6.85 |
| New York Life Insurance Group | -3,027,290 | 4.75 |
| TIAA-CREF | -2,317,339 | 3.63 |
| Western & Southern Mutual Holding Company | -1,364,643 | 2.14 |
| Hartford Financial Services Group | -1,338,845 | 2.10 |
| **2009** | | |
| MetLife, Inc. | $-4,322,365 | 22.51% |
| Hartford Financial Services Group | -3,390,195 | 17.66 |
| American International Group | -2,053,011 | 10.69 |
| Ameriprise Financial, Inc. | -1,837,537 | 9.57 |
| Pacific Mutual Holding Company | -1,150,169 | 5.99 |
| AEGON N.V. | -1,087,585 | 5.66 |

Source: GAO analysis of statutory financial statement data in SNL Financial.
Note: Data are shown in nominal dollars.

Tables 8 and 9 list the P/C insurers with realized and unrealized losses exceeding $1 billion in 2008 and 2009.

**Table 8: Property/Casualty Insurers with $1 Billion or More in Realized Losses, 2008 and 2009**

Dollars in thousands

| Insurer | Realized losses | Percentage of all realized losses |
|---|---|---|
| **2008** | | |
| Ambac Financial Group, Inc. | $-4,371,589 | 17.13% |
| American International Group | -1,697,065 | 6.65 |
| Allstate Corporation | -1,280,299 | 5.02 |
| Hartford Financial Services Group | -1,268,082 | 4.97 |
| CNA Financial Corporation | -1,196,010 | 4.69 |
| Erie Insurance Group | -1,125,560 | 4.41 |
| Berkshire Hathaway, Inc. | -1,036,242 | 4.06 |
| **2009** | | |
| Ambac Financial Group, Inc. | $-3,022,767 | 25.53% |
| Berkshire Hathaway, Inc. | -2,770,133 | 23.40 |

Source: GAO analysis of statutory financial statement data in SNL Financial.

Note: Data are shown in nominal dollars.

**Table 9: Property/Casualty Insurers with $1 Billion or More in Unrealized Losses, 2008 and 2009**

Dollars in thousands

| Insurer | Unrealized losses | Percentage of all unrealized losses |
|---|---|---|
| **2008** | | |
| Berkshire Hathaway, Inc. | $-23,456,610 | 27.41% |
| State Farm Mutual Automobile Insurance Company | -17,182,241 | 20.08 |
| L berty Mutual | -6,193,138 | 7.24 |
| American International Group | -4,014,608 | 4.69 |
| Allstate Corporation | -3,158,281 | 3.69 |
| CNA Financial Corporation | -2,671,781 | 3.12 |
| Nationwide Mutual Group | -1,983,859 | 2.32 |
| Cincinnati Financial Corporation | -1,734,113 | 2.03 |
| Hartford Financial Services | -1,565,621 | 1.83 |
| FM Global | -1,053,450 | 1.23 |

Dollars in thousands

| Insurer | Unrealized losses | Percentage of all unrealized losses |
|---|---|---|
| **2009** | | |
| Nationwide Mutual Group | $-1,998,528 | 47.10% |

Source: GAO analysis of statutory financial statement data in SNL Financial.

Note: Data are shown in nominal dollars.

## Financing Cash Flow

Financing cash flow reflects the extent to which insurers are willing or able to access external capital to finance or grow their operations. It represents the net flow of cash from equity issuance, borrowed funds, dividends to stockholders, and other financing activities. With exceptions in 2004 and 2007 for life insurers and 2005 for P/C insurers, both industries had negative financing cash flows a few years before the crisis began, indicating that insurers were reducing their outstanding debt and equity. These reductions could have resulted from the insurers buying back their stock and not issuing new debt as their existing debt matured. The increasingly negative financing cash flows for both industries starting in 2008 also reflect what we were told about the difficulty of obtaining outside capital during the crisis. Insurers might not have been able to raise money during the crisis even if they had wanted or needed to do so.

Figure 15: Life and Property/Casualty Insurers' Net Cash Flows from Financing and Miscellaneous Sources, 2002-2011

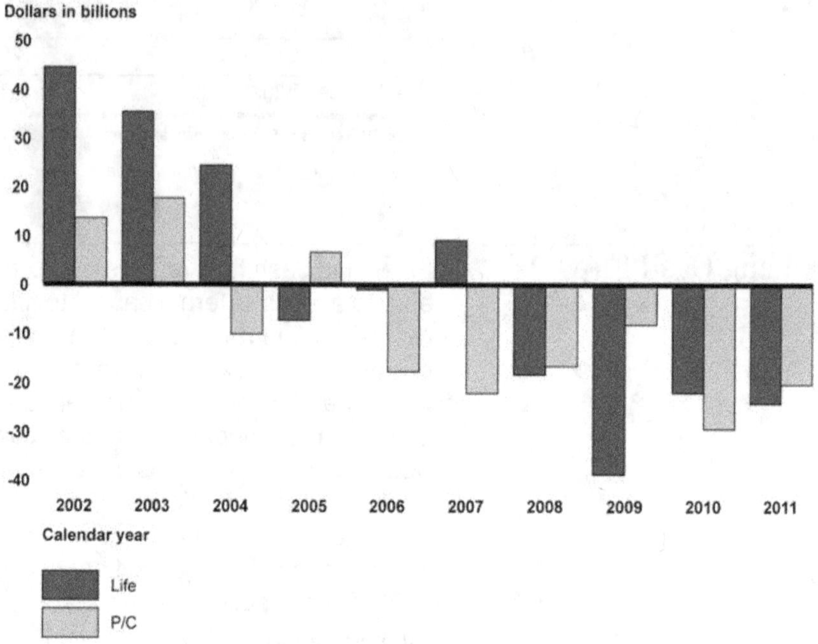

Dollars in billions

Calendar year

Life
P/C

Source: GAO analysis of statutory financial statement data in SNL Financial.

Note: Data are shown in nominal dollars.

## P/C Premium Revenues

In the P/C industry as a whole, net premiums written declined from $443.7 billion in 2006 to $417.5 billion in 2009—a total decline of 6 percent during the crisis years. In most of the lines of P/C insurance that we reviewed, declines in premiums during the crisis were modest (see fig.16). Financial and mortgage guaranty insurance (which combined represent less than 2 percent of the P/C industry)—as well as other liability (occurrence) (insurance against miscellaneous liability due to negligence or improper conduct)—were the exceptions. For example, financial guaranty insurers' net premiums written fell from $3.2 billion in 2008 to $1.8 billion in 2009 (a 43 percent decline). By 2011, net financial guaranty premiums written were less than $1 billion, reflecting a total decline of 69 percent since 2008. Mortgage guaranty insurance premiums fell from $5.4 billion to $4.6 billion (a 14 percent decline) from 2008 to 2009 and to $4.2 billion (another 8 percent decline) in 2010. Net premiums written for other liability (occurrence) declined from $25.9 billion to $24.3 billion (a 6 percent decline) in 2008 and to $20.9 billion (a 14 percent decline) in 2009. On the other hand, net premiums written for homeowners' insurance increased in every year of the 10-year review period, including increases of about 2 percent annually in 2008 and 2009 with net premiums of $56.9 billion in 2009. Net premiums written for all other lines of P/C insurance combined declined from $142.2 billion in 2007 to $129.0 billion in 2009, reflecting annual decreases of less than 1 percent in 2007, 3 percent in 2008, and 7 percent in 2009.[2]

[2]The P/C industry encompasses many lines of insurance. For example, other lines of P/C insurance include—but are not limited to—fire, farmowners, ocean marine, medical professional liability, earthquake, group accident and health, workers' compensation, product liability, commercial auto liability, and credit insurance.

Figure 16: Net Premiums Written for Selected Property/Casualty Lines of Business, 2002-2011

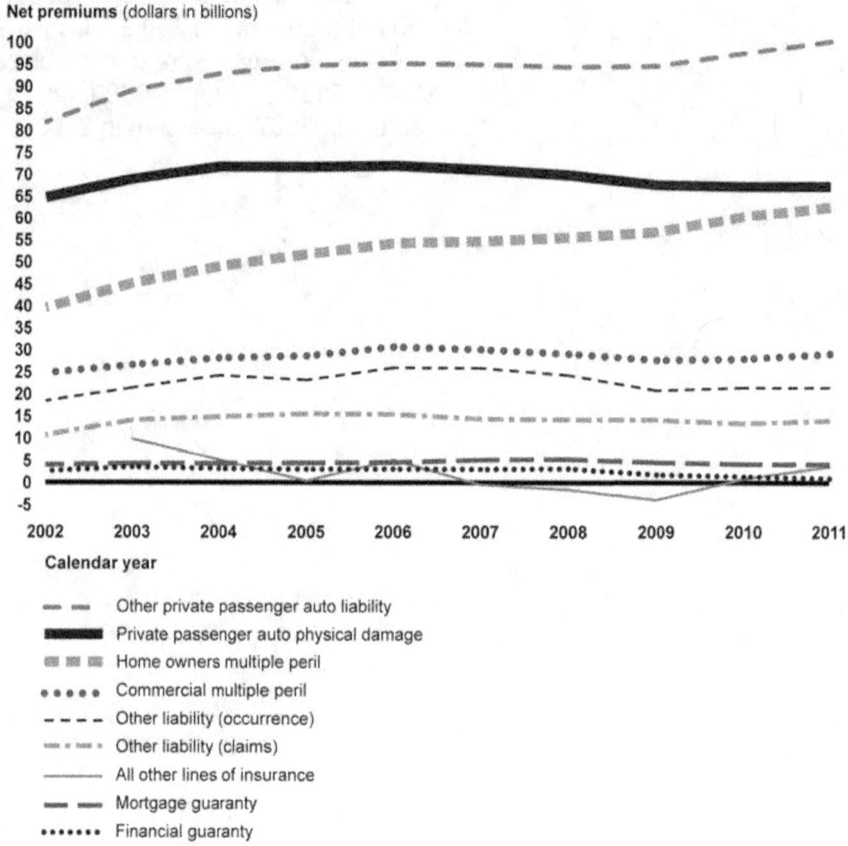
Net premiums (dollars in billions)
100
95
90
85
80
75
70
65
60
55
50
45
40
35
30
25
20
15
10
5
0
-5
2002
2003
2004
2005
2006
2007
2008
2009
2010
2011
Calendar year
Other private passenger auto liability
Private passenger auto physical damage
Home owners multiple peril
Commercial multiple peril
Other liability (occurrence)
Other liability (claims)
All other lines of insurance
Mortgage guaranty
Financial guaranty

Source: GAO analysis of statutory financial statement data in SNL Financial.

Note: Data are shown in nominal dollars.

## Assets and Net Equity of Companies in Liquidation

Based on the available data that NAIC provided us on companies that were liquidated from 2002 through 2011, average assets and net equity of liquidated life and P/C insurers varied by year.[3] As tables 10 and 11 illustrate, average assets of liquidated companies were significantly above the 10-year average in 2004 for the life industry and in 2003 and

[3]NAIC was not able to provide complete financial data for all insurers. The figures in tables 10 and 11 are based on the available data. We have noted the extent to which we were missing financial data for each year. See the Objectives, Scope and Methodology section for further explanation.

2008 for the P/C industry. This was generally due to one or two large companies being liquidated. For example, in 2004, London Pacific Life and Annuity Company was liquidated with $1.5 billion in assets and negative $126 million in net equity, meaning that its liabilities exceeded its assets by that amount. Similarly, MIIX Insurance Company, a P/C insurer, was liquidated in 2008 with assets of $510 million and negative $32 million in net equity. Average net equity, based on the available data, was positive for liquidated life insurers in 2003, 2007, 2009, and 2010 (see table 10). According to NAIC staff, this is not unusual, as regulators typically try to liquidate distressed insurers before their net equity reaches negative levels.

**Table 10: Average Assets and Net Equity (Assets Minus Liabilities) of Life Insurance Companies in Liquidation, 2002-2011**

| Year | Average assets | Median assets | Average net equity | Notes |
|---|---|---|---|---|
| 2002 | $228,832 | $85,492 | ($9,174,419) | Based on financial data available for 4 of 7 companies. |
| 2003 | 355,911 | 355,911 | 287,136 | Based on financial data available for 2 of 4 companies. |
| 2004 | 491,288,146 | 761,126 | (42,340,783) | Based on financial data available for 3 of 5 companies. |
| 2005 | 4,771,020 | 3,113,824 | (2,068,372) | |
| 2006 | 7,563,413 | 5,602,572 | (2,843,453) | |
| 2007 | 25,167,723 | 11,899,542 | 1,331,556 | Average net equity based on financial data available for 2 of 3 companies. |
| 2008 | 92,995,829 | 4,062,709 | (201,581,872) | |
| 2009 | 65,110,752 | 3,432,952 | 7,480,692 | |
| 2010 | 26,472,746 | 11,197,352 | 2,064,663 | |
| 2011 | 37,919,411 | 37,919,411 | (160,962) | |
| 10 year average assets: | $73,347,592 | | | Based on financial data available for 33 of 40 companies. |

Source: GAO analysis of NAIC Global Receivership Information Database data.

Notes:

Data are shown in nominal dollars.

Unless otherwise noted in the "Notes" column, figures reflect data on all liquidations that occurred in a given year.

**Table 11: Average Assets and Net Equity (Assets Minus Liabilities) of Property/Casualty Companies in Liquidation, 2002-2011**

| Year | Average assets | Median assets | Average net equity | Notes |
|---|---|---|---|---|
| 2002 | $16,814,604 | $19,119,524 | ($75,550,387) | Average and median assets based on financial data available for 11 of 16 companies. Average net equity based on financial data available for 6 of 16 companies. |
| 2003 | 365,951,597 | 34,992,852 | (401,800,128) | Average and median assets based on financial data available for 10 of 16 companies. Average net equity based on financial data available for 9 of 16 companies. |
| 2004 | 34,399,196 | 31,518,779 | (16,199,179) | Average and median assets based on financial data available for 10 of 11 companies. Average net equity based on financial data available for 8 of 11 companies. |
| 2005 | 10,441,213 | 10,575,389 | (7,765,547) | Average net equity based on financial data available for 10 of 11 companies. |
| 2006 | 97,118,048 | 37,602,758 | (46,792,277) | Based on financial data available for 11 of 15 companies. |
| 2007 | 8,793,203 | 4,384,739 | (7,155,768) | — |
| 2008 | 130,585,870 | 5,927,680 | (8,913,750) | — |
| 2009 | 12,011,297 | 3,678,951 | (5,093,472) | Based on financial data available for 12 of 13 companies. |
| 2010 | 18,011,525 | 8,334,604 | (8,945,922) | Average and median assets based on financial data available for 14 of 15 companies. Average net equity based on financial data available for 13 of 15 companies. |
| 2011 | 27,943,467 | 10,997,641 | (3,521,801) | Based on financial data available for 16 of 17 companies. |
| **10 year average assets:** | **$64,140,648** | | | Based on financial data available for 106 of 125 companies. |

Source: GAO analysis of NAIC Global Receivership Information Database data.

Notes:

Data are shown in nominal dollars.

Unless otherwise noted in the "Notes" column, figures reflect data on all liquidations that occurred in a given year.

## Stock Prices

We analyzed the monthly closing stock prices of publicly traded life and P/C insurance companies for the period December 2004 through December 2011. We used two A.M. Best indexes—the A.M. Best U.S. Life Index and the A.M. Best Property Casualty Index—as a proxy for the life and P/C industries. According to A.M. Best, the indexes include all U.S. insurance industry companies that are publicly traded on major global stock exchanges that also have an A.M. Best rating, or that have an insurance subsidiary with an A.M. Best rating. They are based on the aggregation of the prices of the individual publicly traded stocks and weighted for their respective free float market capitalizations. The life index represents 21 life insurance companies and the P/C index represents 56 P/C companies. Since more than 60 percent of the companies on the A.M. Best indexes we selected trade on NYSE, we also obtained monthly closing stock prices on the New York Stock Exchange (NYSE) Composite Index, which, as of February 2012, represented 1,867 companies that trade on NYSE, to provide a contextual perspective on the overall stock market during our review period.

As figure 17 illustrates, life and P/C insurers' aggregate stock prices generally moved in tandem with the larger NYSE Composite Index from the end of 2004 through 2011, but life insurers' aggregate stock prices fell much more steeply in late 2008 and early 2009 than P/C insurers' and NYSE companies' aggregate stock prices.

**Figure 17: Month-End Closing Stock Levels for Publicly Traded Life and Property/Casualty Companies and NYSE Companies, December 2004-December 2011**

Source: GAO analysis of A.M. Best data on the A.M. Best U.S. Life and Property Casualty Indexes and the New York Stock Exchange Composite Index.

Notes:

According to A.M. Best, the A.M. Best U.S. Life and Property Casualty Insurance Indexes provide a benchmark for assessing investor confidence that often correlates with general financial performance of the overall insurance industry, a specific insurance business segment, and specific companies in the context of their business segments. The indexes include all insurance industry companies that are publicly traded on major global stock exchanges that also have an interactive Best's rating, or that have an insurance subsidiary with an interactive Best's rating. They are based on the aggregation of the prices of the individual publicly traded stocks and weighted for their respective free float market capitalizations. The life index represents 21 life insurance companies and the P/C index represents 56 P/C companies. The NYSE Composite Index represents more than 1,800 companies that trade on the New York Stock Exchange.

The left vertical axis represents the basis for the A.M. Best life and P/C Indexes; they are based on an index value of 1,000 as of December 31, 2004, when A.M. Best established the indexes. The right vertical axis is the basis for the NYSE Composite Index, which is based on an index value of 5,000 as of December 31, 2002, when a new methodology for the index took effect. We overlaid the lines to more effectively compare changes in the indexes over time.

We selected several key time periods or events from the financial crisis and identified the largest drops in life and P/C insurers' aggregate stock prices during those time periods (see fig.18). While many factors can affect the daily movement of stock prices, we observed that changes in life insurers' aggregate stock prices tended to be more correlated with several of the events that occurred during the crisis than P/C insurers' aggregate stock prices.

**Figure 18: Key Events in the Financial Crisis and Stock Indices for Publicly Traded Life and Property/Casualty Insurers for 2007**

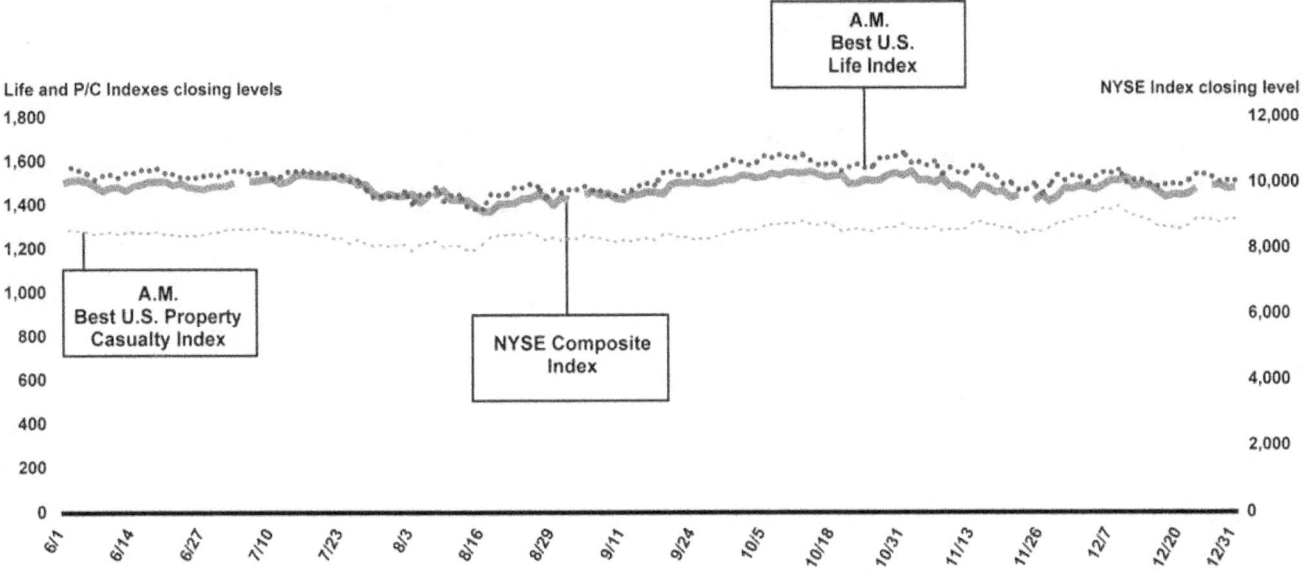

◉ Fall of 2007

As conditions in the U.S. housing market deteriorate, American International Group Financial Products Corporation begins to lose massive amounts of money on credit default swaps issued on collaterized debt obligations.

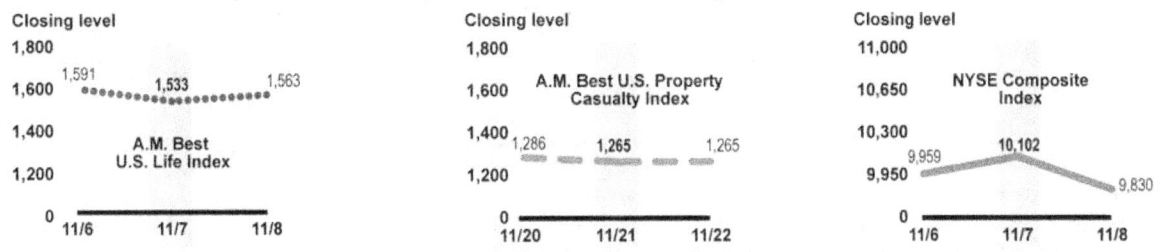

Source: GAO analysis of A.M. Best data on the A.M. Best U.S. Life and Property Casualty Indexes and the New York Stock Exchange Composite Index.

**Figure 19: Key Events in the Financial Crisis and Stock Indices for Publicly Traded Life and Property/Casualty Insurers for 2008**

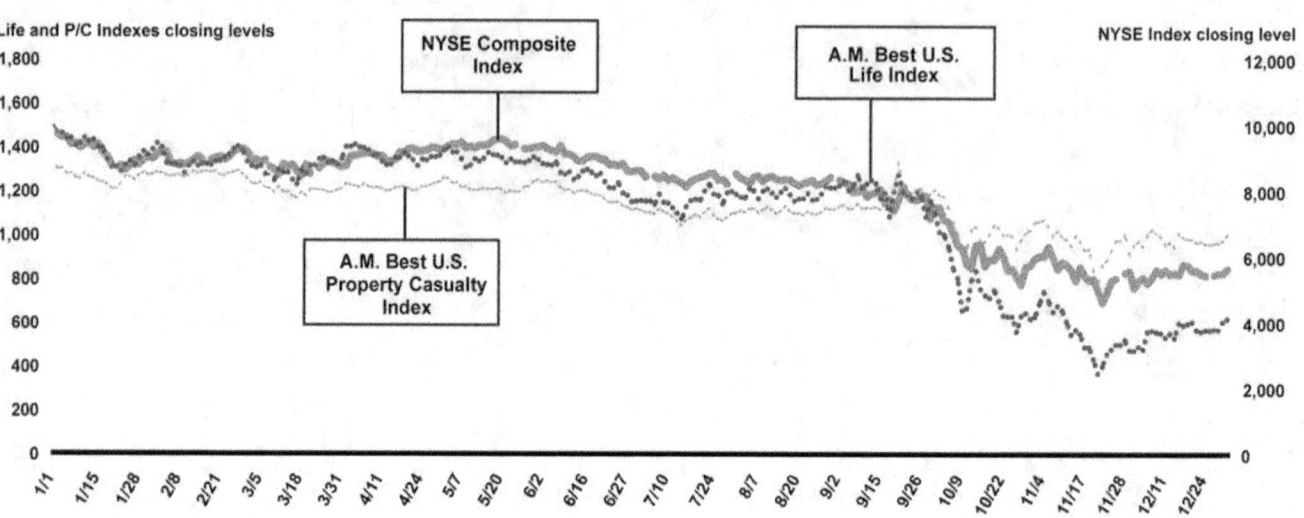

● **February-March 2008**

In March 2008, the Federal Reserve Bank of New York extends credit to Bear Stearns through JP Morgan Chase Bank to address their immediate liquidity needs and forestall the potential systemic disruptions of a default or bankruptcy.

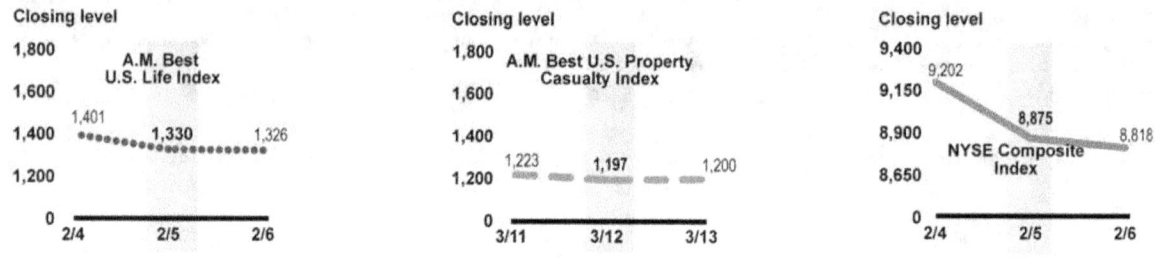

● **May-June 2008**

In May 2008, credit ratings agencies Standard & Poor's, Fitch Ratings, and Moody's Investor Services each downgrade their ratings on AIG.

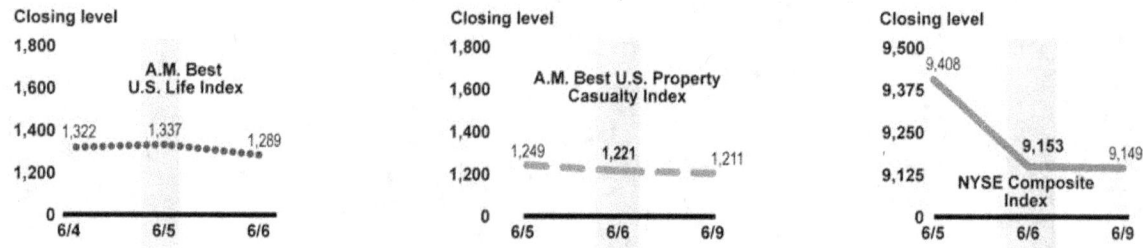

Source: GAO analysis of A.M. Best data on the A.M. Best U.S. Life and Property Casualty Indexes and the New York Stock Exchange Composite Index.

Figure 20: Key Events in the Financial Crisis and Stock Indices for Publicly Traded Life and Property/Casualty Insurers for 2009

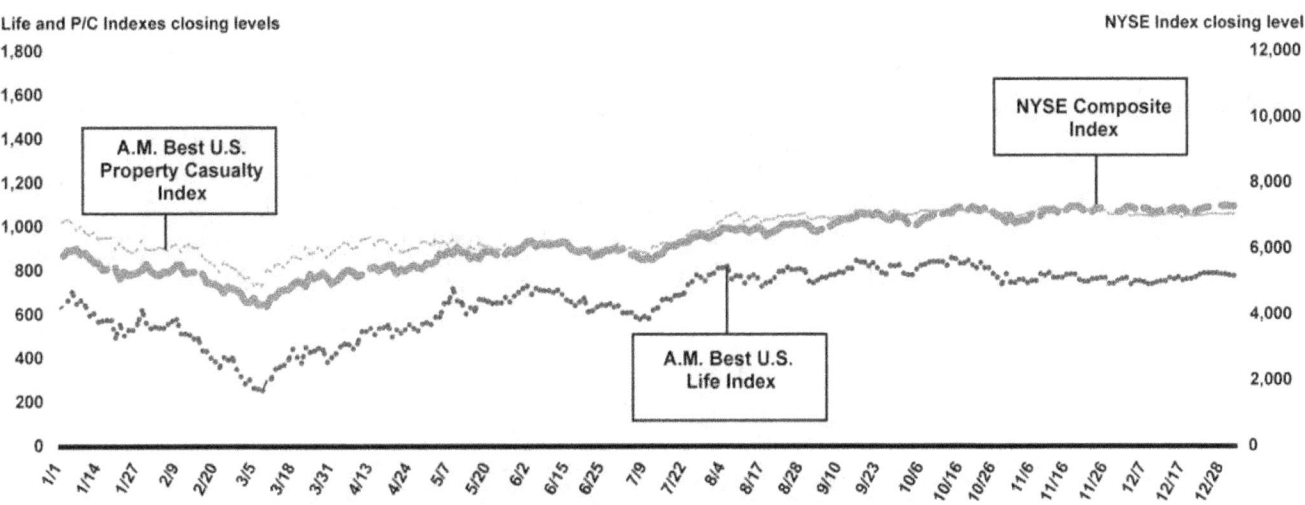

⊙ May 2009
The federal government continues to provide assistance to financial institutions such as the Federal Reserve's Term Asset-Backed Securities Loan Facility and the U.S. Treasury's Capital Purchase Program.

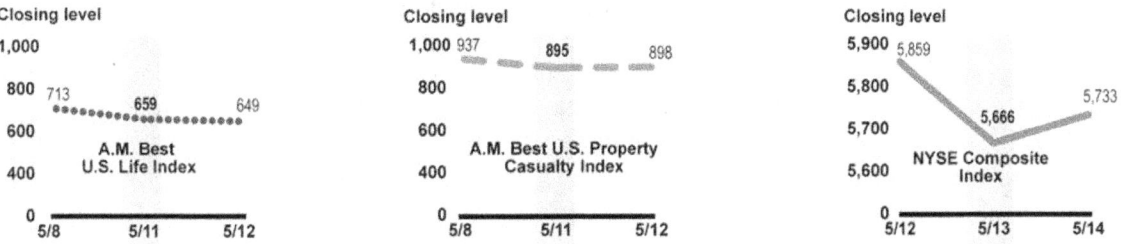

Source: GAO analysis of A.M. Best data on the A.M. Best U.S. Life and Property Casualty Indexes and the New York Stock Exchange Composite Index.

# Appendix III: Profiles of Distressed Insurers

This appendix provides more detail on two distressed insurers—one mortgage guaranty insurer and one life insurer—during the financial crisis.[1]

## Mortgage Guaranty Insurer

We studied a mortgage guaranty insurer operating in a run-off of its existing book of business (that is, it had ceased writing new mortgage guaranty business and was only servicing the business it already had on its books). This insurer is licensed in all states and the District of Columbia. Prior to its run-off, the insurer provided mortgage default protection to lenders on an individual loan basis and on pools of loans. As a result of continued losses stemming from defaults of mortgage loans, the state regulator placed the insurer into rehabilitation with a finding of insolvency in 2012.[2]

During the financial crisis, the insurer began experiencing substantial losses due to increasing default rates on insured mortgages, particularly in California, Florida, Arizona, and Nevada. As table 12 shows, in 2007 and 2008, over 30 percent of the insurer's underwritten risk—the total amount of coverage for which it was at risk under its certificates of insurance—was originated in these distressed markets, which experienced default rates that peaked at more than 35 percent in 2009. In addition, the insurer had significant exposure to Alt-A loans, which are loans that were issued to borrowers based on credit scores but without documentation of the borrowers' income, assets, or employment. These loans experienced higher default rates than the prime fixed-rate loans in the insurer's portfolio.

---

[1] Although we used court documents to compile the profiles, we refrained from citing them in order to maintain the two insurers' anonymity.

[2] In rehabilitation, a court gives the state insurance regulator the authority to manage a financially troubled insurer until its problems are corrected. A finding of insolvency means that an insurer is unable to meet its liabilities.

**Table 12: Distressed Market Default Rates and Percentage of Insurer's Total Underwritten Risk, 2007-2011**

| Calendar Year | Default rate in distressed markets | Coverage in distressed markets as percentage of insurer's total underwritten risk |
|---|---|---|
| 2007 | 5.7% | 32.1% |
| 2008 | 22.7 | 34.4 |
| 2009 | 35.4 | 25.2 |
| 2010 | 29.9 | 23.5 |
| 2011 | 26.9 | 22.1 |

Source: GAO analysis of insurer's annual Form 10-K filings.

This insurer rapidly depleted its capital as it set aside reserves to meet obligations resulting from the overall rising volume of mortgage defaults. Rising defaults combined with unsuccessful attempts to raise additional capital during the crisis adversely affected its statutory risk-to-capital ratio starting in 2008. While state insurance regulations generally require this relationship of insured risk to statutory capital (in this case, the sum of statutory surplus and contingency reserves) to be no greater than 25 to 1, this insurer's statutory capital declined 85 percent from year-end 2007 to year-end 2008, increasing the risk-to-capital ratio from 21 to 1 to 125 to 1.[3] As a result, in 2008, this insurer entered into an order with its state regulator to cease writing new business and operate in run-off status. Due to continued increases in mortgage defaults, the regulator required a capital maintenance plan in 2009 that allowed the insurer to maintain a positive statutory capital position during the run-off and also to pay partial claims.

According to court filings, the insurer reported to the state regulator that its liabilities outweighed its assets by more than $800 million for the second quarter of 2012. As a result, the state regulator entered an order with the relevant county circuit court in late 2012 to take the insurer into rehabilitation with a finding of insolvency. At that time, the court named the state insurance regulator as rehabilitator, which means that it gave

---

[3]Policyholders' surplus is the excess of an insurance company's assets above its legal obligations to meet the benefits (liabilities) payable to its policyholders. Mortgage guaranty insurers must set aside 50 percent of unearned premiums remaining after establishment of their unearned premium reserve in a contingency reserve. The contingency reserve is meant to protect policyholders against the effects of adverse economic cycles.

the regulator authority over the insurer's property, business, and affairs until the insurer's problems are corrected.

## Life Insurer

We studied a life insurer that primarily writes life, annuity, and accident and health business. Due to losses sustained from equity investments in Fannie Mae and Freddie Mac in 2008, the state regulator placed the insurer in rehabilitation in early 2009.[4] In late 2011, the regulator approved of the insurer's acquisition by a third-party insurer. This transaction facilitated the insurer's successful exit from rehabilitation in mid-2012.

The insurer was invested in Fannie Mae and Freddie Mac stock. In 2008, the insurer sustained approximately $95 million in investment losses. Approximately $47 million of those investment losses were related to investments in Fannie Mae and Freddie Mac stock. These events adversely affected the insurer's capital, which declined by over 38 percent from March 31, 2008 to September 30, 2008.[5] As of December 31, 2008, the insurer had capital of $29 million, down from about $126 million as of December 31, 2007.

Due to the rapid deterioration of its financial condition, the court placed the insurer into rehabilitation in early 2009. According to testimony by a member of the receivership team, at the time of the order of rehabilitation, the insurer had a net liability of $118 million on a liquidation basis.[6] In receivership, the regulator granted the insurer an exemption from a state insurance statute restricting certain types of investments based on a

---

[4]Fannie Mae and Freddie Mac are government-sponsored enterprises that were established to provide liquidity, stability, and affordability in the secondary market for both single- and multifamily mortgages. They purchase mortgages that meet their underwriting standards from primary mortgage lenders, such as banks or thrifts, and either hold the mortgages in their portfolios or package them into mortgage-backed securities (MBS).

[5]On September 6, 2008, the Federal Housing Finance Agency (FHFA) placed Fannie Mae and Freddie Mac into conservatorship out of concern that their deteriorating financial condition would destabilize the financial system.

[6]This means that the company assumed that policies would have been voluntarily surrendered by all policyholders and that those policyholders would therefore, have had to pay surrender charges on those policies. Alternatively, according to the receivership team member's testimony, if the company had assumed that policyholders would have been compelled to surrender their policies rather than doing so voluntarily, the deficit would have been approximately $190 million.

company's surplus and asset levels. According to the testimony, this exemption allowed the insurer to report capital of $400,000 instead of a $259 million deficit as of December 31, 2009.

In late 2009, the receiver issued a request for proposal for the sale of the insurer. By mid-2010, the receiver was in negotiations with another life insurance group. In 2011, policyholders and the receiver approved of a purchase plan. The plan would recapitalize the insurer to allow it sufficient surplus to meet state minimum requirements to resume writing new business. The plan was executed in mid-2012, which allowed the insurer to exit rehabilitation.

# Appendix IV: GAO Contact and Staff Acknowledgments

| | |
|---|---|
| **GAO Contact** | Alicia Puente Cackley, (202) 512-8678 or cackleya@gao.gov |
| **Staff Acknowledgments** | In addition to the contact named above, Patrick A. Ward (Assistant Director), Emily R. Chalmers, William R. Chatlos, Janet Fong, David J. Lin, Angela Pun, Lisa M. Reynolds, Jessica M. Sandler, and Jena Y. Sinkfield made significant contributions to this report. |

Please Print on Recycled Paper.